A Friend in Every City
—— One Global Family ——

A Networking Vision for the Twenty-First Century

Penny Power
Thomas Power

with Andy Coote

A Friend in Every City
© Penny Power, Thomas Power, Andy Coote 2006

Cover design: Simon May, Ideas of the Mind
Author Photos: Richard Brayshaw (Penny and Thomas)
and Martin Coote (Andy)
Page design and setting: Jaquetta Trueman, Graphic Solutions
Book text set in Myriad Pro Regular 11 on 14pt
First published in 2006 by Ecademy Press

Contact:
Ecademy Press
6, Woodland Rise
Penryn, Cornwall, UK
TR10 8QD

info@ecademy-press.com

Printed and Bound by Lightning Source UK and USA

Contents

 *About the Authors*

Penny Power

As a child, Penny Ross wanted nothing more than to be involved in a caring profession. So, at 18, whilst waiting to go to college to study to be a carer, she took a temporary job working in a telesales department. It was not an auspicious beginning.

"I spent three weeks applying lipstick to give me confidence before each call, my lips grew but my confidence reduced, I was pretending to talk to customers at the end of the phone when I cold called, it was alien to my personality. Then one day a poor unsuspecting prospect actually had to talk to me. I apologised for disturbing him, sympathised with the fact that he had a sore throat and said I would ring him another day. At lunchtime, I went to buy my sandwich and saw some Tunes (cough sweets) on the counter. I bought them and sent them to 'the poor man on the phone' wishing him a speedy recovery. Three days later he phoned in to place a huge order." Penny learnt that, if you create the right environment and are a giving person, you can receive, rather than having to ask. From then on, she built her career through her relationships and her attitude of caring for others, whether they were staff, suppliers, customers or colleagues.

Penny remained in the IT Industry until she stopped to have her family with her husband Thomas in 1992. As Sales and Marketing director of an IT company, Nicole Wehden (a consultant Penny used), remembers Penny as very committed, hard-working, caring, a giving person, sharing, supportive and keen to build friendship and trust. Penny always imagined that one day she would re-invent herself and start a career in a more vocational way once she had a break to start her family.

Penny concentrated on bringing up her three children and supporting Thomas in his development as a speaker and consultant. In 1998 Penny came up with the idea of Ecademy, a Social Business Network to connect business people for learning, career and business development.

In the early days of Ecademy, Penny was combining her family life with the development of the initial website and the business. Glenn Watkins joined Penny right at the beginning becoming Chief Executive in 2001. Glenn built the business whilst Thomas took over as the front person for Ecademy. Penny spent time bringing up the children, remaining in the background of Ecademy, but always watching and contacting members.

In 2005, when her children were 13, 11 and 8, Penny returned to the forefront of Ecademy, hosting the monthly London meetings and heading an Asian tour meeting Ecademy members in Kuala Lumpur, Singapore, Jakarta and Bali. Penny still combines her work life with her family life – the children are very involved in the business and know many of the members, and they also travelled with Penny during her 2005 tour.

Penny has also been developing her thinking around Emotional Wealth during 2005 with a view to helping more Ecademy members discover their true passion and to communicate it effectively to achieve real network value.

Thomas Power

Thomas is Chairman and co-Founder of Ecademy. As such he is involved at the heart of the changing way we are doing business in the 21st Century.

His 2003 book, *Networking for Life*, sets out some of his key beliefs about doing business in an increasingly freelance world.

Thomas believes that networking will be THE key skill for business people in the 21st Century. He believes that, as more of the working populations of the Western economies become self employed, it will be a case of 'network or starve'. So many people find, as they move voluntarily or otherwise from the corporate world into self-employment that their WorkNet – the people they work with, within and external to their corporate role – completely fails to support them and that they need a network. Ecademy has been developed to help such people adjust to their new circumstances, receive support and find their place in the new working environment.

Thomas is the ultimate connector. He has met over 23,000 people since 1982 and continues to hold regular one-to-one meetings. His detailed memory allows him to connect people together based only on information that he learns in meetings and from Ecademy profiles.

Thomas wants Ecademy to provide wealth for its members. Emotional Wealth, he believes, comes first from who you are and what you stand for, while Financial Wealth comes from what you do. As Thomas notes in his Ecademy profile, "we believe that to achieve success in business, people should focus first on the emotional side of their lives and let the financial or transactional side reveal itself once the emotional side is securely in place. It is all about relationships first and transactions second".

Thomas is non Executive Director of FTSE Tracker 1000 company QXL plc and sees the changing world of work from both sides.

He sees self employment within a series of Networks in effect superseding Corporations as the next evolution of business over, perhaps, the next 30 years. "I call these vehicles SENs or SEMPs i.e. self-employed networks. I have not found another term for them.

There will be tens of thousands of SENs. Ecademy is only one, and a fledgling one at that. There are already hundreds of others you might wish to examine or join".

"There is no doubt in my mind that random groups of people thrown together in unstructured networks can outperform any aggregrated homogeneous corporation. We are yet to see, however, how such a self-employed network will operate. By 2010 forecasters believe 50% of the US economy will be self-employed. Only after then will we begin to see the rise of the self-employed network (SEN)."

His down-to-earth speaking style and the wealth of content he has to call upon make him a popular speaker. His combative and controversial style inspires his audiences to rethink their current strategies for marketing to include networking, even to place it at the forefront of their thinking.

Andy Coote

Andy is a freelance writer and editor. He recently set up Ecademy Press with Mindy Gibbins-Klein and is working in partnership with Ecademy to deliver books that interest the growing community of networkers around the globe.

His background includes a short spell as a policeman, several years in retail as an Information Technologist and nearly 10 years selling IT solutions to business. In 2001, having spent three years of self employment learning to cope with stress-related illness, Andy decided to make a change in his life and become a full-time writer. He joined the Falmouth College of Arts Post Graduate Diploma in Professional Writing and spent an academic year writing in a variety of styles and genres.

On his return from full-time education, Andy set up Bizwords as a vehicle for his writing and began marketing himself through his network. This led to some work, including teaching work on E-Commerce at Cardiff Business School, and some magazine feature writing with SC Magazine on Information Security issues. He also spent over a year as the newsletter editor for the Alliance of Business Consultants (ABC).

His networking grew through Business X-Change, Business Link Wessex's networking initiative, Andover Mutual Business Group and ABC. There was, however, something missing. It was possible to go to meetings, have productive conversations and leave fully intending to do something to follow up, but somehow nothing actually did happen.

In October 2003, Andy was invited to join Ecademy. He joined, with no expectations that online networking would work for him and found that it, in fact, addressed the very problem he had with networking events. Between events, members could connect with each other and continue the conversations started at events. He attended clubs in Hampshire and Surrey, putting in the miles to meet people and develop relationships.

In March, 2004, Andy set up Test Valley Ecademy for Andover and Romsey, with Thomas as the main speaker on the launch night in early April. In preparation for this, Andy booked time with Thomas in London for a one-to-one meeting. That meeting was life changing and led, through a guide for Ecademy club leaders, to this collaboration. There was an immediate rapport between Thomas and Andy.

In November, 2004, Andy moved to Cornwall, using Ecademy as a route to finding connections in Cornwall prior to the move. He still keeps in touch with connections across Southern England and around the world and is actively looking to grow his network. He makes frequent visits to events in London, visited Bali for an event in 2005 and is looking to expand his international networking in 2006. Many connections made at Ecademy have already turned into friendships.

Andy became one of the first wave of Life Members of Ecademy in December, 2004, and has found a great group of like-minded people with whom to network. Ecademy Press was one idea that came into existence because of fellow life-members (known as BlackStars).

Acknowledgements

This book has been a collaboration between the three authors and a wider group of helpers and advisors. A number of people were interviewed but, in the event, are not directly quoted in the book. Their input was valuable in shaping the ideas and concepts in the book.

Glenn Watkins, Chief Executive of Ecademy has been instrumental in the development of this book. Also specific thanks go to Paul Sherman, Julian Bond and Andrew Widgery at Ecademy. Thanks also to Heather-Jane Sears, Simon Rogers, Nicole Wehden, Allison McSparron-Edwards, Ronald Wopereis, Tom Evans, Nick Heap, Steve Murphy, Roger Hamilton and Alan Rae who contributed to the research. Nicola Cooper-Abbs expertly edited the text – any remaining errors are ours, not hers. William Buist and Judith Germain also read the text and provided valuable feedback. Martin Ley at Em-Dash Publications and Jaquetta Trueman at Graphic Solutions indexed and typeset the book.

To those people and to everyone else we've pestered or plundered for material for this book, we give our heartfelt thanks.

In a book with three authors, there has been some debate about how to introduce ideas. Some are introduced by name – ' Thomas Power suggests' or ' Penny sees it this way' - whilst others can be attributed to us as a group in which case 'we' and 'us' will be used.

In referring to non-specific people in the text, the words he and she, his and hers are used randomly and do not imply any gender-specific bias.

Entrepreneur Business School, Bali

I n late September 2005, a key stage in the writing of this book, Penny, Thomas and Andy arrived in Bali within sight of the holy temple at Tanah Lot. They arrived separately, at the end of their quite distinct personal journeys.

Penny had been touring Malaysia, Singapore and Indonesia with Roger Hamilton and talking to networking groups about Ecademy and why emotional wealth is so important. Her message, about emotional wealth and the power of networking was well received in Kuala Lumpur, Singapore and Jakarta.

Thomas, meanwhile, had been resting and relaxing on Bali with their three children. This had been a role reversal as Penny re-emerged as a speaker for and about Ecademy.

Andy's journey was from London via Kuala Lumpur. This was to be a short break from the research and writing of this book.

In Bali it was hot, and busy. The people were friendly and the most dangerous activity seemed to be being driven on the bustling Balinese roads given the numbers of vehicles, especially motor cycles, on the road.

We were in Bali to take part in the Entrepreneur Business School, 2005 organised by XL Results Foundation and hosted by Roger

Hamilton, founder of XL, who also runs the Asia-Pacific network for Ecademy.

Our roles were very different. Thomas and Penny were there to mentor teams competing to win the Bali Challenge on how to develop Network Value as part of a viable and socially responsible business plan. Thomas had done this before, and easily donned the persona of Simon Cowell – just try to impress him! Penny was mentoring for the first time. She found the balance between challenge and support stressful. Her natural instinct is to support everyone and she did this in person-to-person talks with many of the 120 participants from across the world.

Andy's role was to ride the roller coaster. He was participating and finding the highs and lows of building a team under constant pressure only too real. If he imagined that it was a game that he could sail through, observe and be unchanged by, then he was wrong to do that. Building teams is "not about the plan" as Roger Hamilton repeatedly reminded us. It is about the vulnerability and strength of individuals forging themselves together to become a single unit and making extraordinary things happen. This is truly the Ecademy ideal of 'Connecting Business People'. The best connections were (and still are) founded at an emotional level.

Le Meridien Nirwana resort is on the West Coast of Bali within walking and viewing distance of the Hindu temple of Tanah Lot. Roger told the story of Tanah Lot. It was built around the year 1500 on a rock in the sea and stands intact some 500 years later. Tanah means earth and Lot sea — earth from sea or something from nothing. Today's entrepreneurs have to make something from nothing to succeed. They are the modern-day alchemists. When it all works well, magic happens.

Before our eyes, viable businesses began to emerge from what had been, mostly, raw or sketchy ideas at the start. All of the teams exhibited signs of the classic process of team develop-ment articulated in 1965 by Bruce Tuckman – Forming, Norming, Storming and Performing. Much of the storming happened on

Sunday night (the end of the second full day) and by midday on Monday some of the better performing teams from the early stages seemed to have lost an edge. Other, until that point, poorer performers suddenly found the accelerator.

It was an exercise in understanding the power of and the need for teams to take the entrepreneur's 'something' and make it into a product or service that customers would buy. To do that, the mentor team at EBS suggested that six key values needed development. These were enterprise value, customer value, network value, partnership value, investment value and systems value. In today's market, a seventh, social value may also be needed.

The teams came from many nations and cultures yet worked closely together, developing friendships that will last, some of them forever. Those friendships will be developed online by e-mail and through Ecademy. We look forward to Bali 2006 and to other opportunities to get together again with our friends in many cities around the world.

It was easy to get carried away with the euphoria of so many people from such diverse backgrounds working together. The proof that we still have a long way to go to find harmony and peace in our world was not long in coming. It doesn't negate our hopes for a better world but it does put them into stark perspective. We keep on building friends across the world person by person, conversation by conversation while recognising that a relatively small group of people can disrupt that process – as they did only days after the EBS. If we needed a reality check, this was it!

On Saturday 1st October, 2005, after most of the EBS people had returned home, terrorism and carnage returned to the beautiful island and its gentle people. Bombs in Kuta and Jimbaran Beach killed at least 20 and injured dozens more. In minutes, Bali was contemplating further loss of life and limb and another loss of tourism and confidence like that of 2002.

A dark cloud hangs over Bali again.

What this tells us is that it takes a lot of people to build something strong and worthwhile, but only a very few determined people are needed to destroy it.

 *Introduction*

Why 'A Friend in Every City'?

You're travelling. Perhaps it's only a short journey – London to Birmingham. Maybe New York to Washington. Even a longer journey – London to Sydney or New York to Tokyo. As you arrive you remind yourself of all the good travel advice you've heard. How to avoid cheating taxis, which stations or subway lines to avoid, your best route to your hotel. If you are like the majority of people, this may also be the moment you begin to feel lonely. It's a natural feeling, you're alone in a strange city and we all fear the unfamiliar.

Now change the scene. You arrive at the airport and there, amongst the waiting greeters, is your name on a card and holding the card is your friend. She will guide you back into the city and introduce you to her friends. Maybe you already know some of them. Feeling better already?

When Thomas Power was travelling and expecting to arrive alone, he had those thoughts. Maybe you've thought the same thing? But Thomas Power was already building a social business network called Ecademy. He wanted it to be international and now he knew he wanted it to provide its members with 'a friend in every city'. So the goal was set. As we write this in late 2005 and early 2006, Ecademy is growing quickly. From its UK roots it is spreading across the world. When Rod Wood went to South America in 2004, Ecademy friends were there to help him find new contacts and build new business. The same is true of 150 countries worldwide. Ecademy has members there who espouse the Ecademy ethos of 'winning by sharing'.

Why a friend rather than a contact? Because the unique mixture of social and business contact and the third-party rating systems allow a trust to develop between contacts. It might not happen every time but it frequently does – which leads to friendship often before, or without, meeting. As friendship leads to trust, so trust leads to trade. The other members of Ecademy may not be your customers but they will know people who could be. They are your door openers – your route to market.

It's a great formula and it works, but only in the right sequence; the relationship must come first and it may lead to friendship and to business.

The title of this book 'A Friend in Every City' is carefully chosen. It talks about networking – so why didn't we choose 'A Contact in Every City' or 'A Business Partner in Every City'? It is because we believe that, as friends, we can be contacts and business partners on a much more intimate level.

What do we mean by friends? From childhood, we have made friends at a number of levels. Friends with whom we would walk to the shops or school, smoking friends sharing an illicit cigarette behind the bike sheds, drinking friends to share a night out, travelling friends to holiday with, neighbourhood friends to meet and greet in the street and business friends that we work with or do deals with.

Some friends will be left behind as we grow and develop our path, our journey. Others stay with us as we change, and we find new friends along the way. A few will become close friends with whom we can share intimate experiences. We move through stages of friendship with some – encounter, companionship, comradeship, togetherness, total intimacy – stopping at the place where we feel most comfortable. With others we go straight to intimacy – we feel that we have encountered a 'kindred spirit'. This mutual resonance can be experienced online, but will be vastly reinforced by face-to-face meeting.

So we might deduce that friendship needs trust to flourish. The opposite position, that trust always needs friendship, is less simple to prove. However, it can be said that if we know that we can trust our friends, it is a good idea to have friends rather than just contacts.

Roger Hamilton refers to levels of power in his work on Wealth Dynamics (see Chapter 13). Elected power comes from your own efforts and must be recharged frequently. Connected power comes from your network and is always there and available for you to tap into. Reflected power comes from a network of friends and is there at all times – giving strength and purpose.

We all need the reassurance and confirmation that we are normal – that we are human – and that can only come from friends. Friends give feedback that is often difficult to accept but always from a good and caring place. They hold up a mirror to show you how you are seen and how you might improve that image.

Having a friend in every city means that you will be less lonely when travelling, more diverse in your thinking, more open to diversity in the world, more open-minded. It offers warmth and safety for you, and creates the potential for a more peaceful world. It has the potential to create a web of peace around the world. Effecting a change for the good of individuals may also lead to creating a change for the good of humanity.

To embrace these changes to our personal journeys, we need to concentrate less on developing our WorkNet – the group of people inside a company whose support mostly goes when you leave – and more on our Network – the support outside of your company (and some insiders) who will stay with you and support you in the long term.

What is in the Book?

The 21st century poses a number of challenges to us that will change to way we work. These include the growth of China and India, along with other eastern nations, as places to outsource work that was formerly done in the West, a general move towards smaller corporate structures based around a core, a crisis in the funding of pensions leading to a need to work longer and a growth in portfolio and freelance working. Chapter 1 expands on these themes to set the scene for the growth of networks.

Chapter 2 examines the key elements of successful Internet businesses. They are matching engines of various types. Matching is a very useful mechanism that will help us to survive the changes we describe in Chapter 1.

Networks have developed over a long while. Indeed, it can be argued that getting together with others is something we have always done, but the connectivity of the internet and improvements in technology generally have led to an explosion of online networks. In Chapter 3, we look at the market for social and business networks and examine a few of those in more detail.

On 7th February1998, Ecademy was founded as a network for e-business professionals. Over time it has developed into a social business network with the tagline 'Connecting Business People'. Chapter 5 tells the story of Ecademy and examines its purpose and principles.

Networks play several different roles in 21st century life. Chapter 6 looks at the development of Social Capital and Citizen Journalism. Networking and Global Labour Matching is the main thrust of Chapter 7, which also looks at Innovation and Entrepreneurship in a network context. Networks create different issues of leadership and management from hierarchies and this is discussed in Chapter 8, with Chapter 9 looking at the place of causes on the Internet and how networks might help them to gain coverage.

From Chapter 10, the focus moves from the networks themselves to the process of networking. Having set the scene for networking, Chapter 11 looks at how to use your profile on various networks to build reputation. Chapter 12 takes a look at personal development and profiling tools for communicating where you are and what you can do more easily. One tool, used by Ecademy in the BlackStar Life Membership context is Wealth Dynamics and, with permission from the owner Roger Hamilton of XL Corporation, Chapter 13 sets out some of the key concepts of this approach to team building and personal understanding.

Chapter 14 concentrates on building a network, looking at the science and art of the process and examining the role of quality and quantity in creating a successful set of connections. With technology tools improving all the time, it is now possible to be a publisher without significant outlay. Good content will still be noticed more than poorer material. Blogging, podcasting and vodcasting are all examined, in Chapter 15, as ways of getting noticed in the noise that is the Internet. Grouping together with others who share an interest or who live in your geographical area is a productive way of getting to know people well. Chapter 16 looks at clubs as online and offline opportunities and puts forward the proposal that, in the next few years, many of us will create clubs that help us to build our own brand and deliver our products and services. For many of us, this will involve the creation of a chargeable club.

The story of networks and networking doesn't stop here. There will be changes and developments throughout the coming years. Chapter 17 looks at the potential of networks to continue to develop useful services and at Ecademy's plans for development through to 2050. The story comes full circle by taking the concept of 'A Friend in Every City' and considers whether, by meeting as friends, networkers can begin to make inroads into the fear and misunderstanding that besets our world. Can networks change the world? If they can, it will be by applying networking approaches person by person, conversation by conversation.

Living and Working in the Twenty-First Century

Halfway through the first decade of the twenty-first century, the world seems poised for a profound change. The Western nations, for so long the manufacturing and economic powerhouses, are being challenged by Eastern economies like China and India. Birth rates are falling worldwide and we are all, on average, living longer. These changes threaten the current Western economic conditions where the retired live longer than previous generations and, in general, have a good standard of living. This cannot continue, and we will see significant changes to the working lives and prosperity of future generations. Creating enough to live on will depend on what and, crucially, who we know. Retirement may become more a dream than a reality for most of us as we struggle to fund our longer life.

A Personal Journey

From the moment of birth we start our journey with one clear destination but no timetable and no predetermined maps. To begin with, our path is charted by our parents and our family and then by our schools. At this stage, authority figures also provide a measure of protection.

After school we may move on to college or enter the world of work. Here we find things are still well mapped out for us. We begin what is called a career. The word implies something smooth and managed, that arcs clearly and effectively from our early days through our most productive years and then settles towards retirement. Retirement is a time to do all those things that your career meant you weren't able to do before. You can do them because you deferred some of your income and you put it into a pension that will keep you, comfortably, until you die.

Sound a little idyllic? Well, today's truth is that, if it ever worked like that, it no longer does.

Sooner or later, for most of us, the map will run out, the protective layer will be stripped away, jobs will not be 'for life' and the pension we've contributed to all our working lives will prove to be less elastic than we expected. We will have to take control of our lives. Better we do it sooner rather than later.

We are all on our personal journey through life and every personal journey intersects with many others. Each intersection offers alternative ways to continue the journey from that point. We reach many intersections and make many choices every day. Choices that can take us forward or set us back. It is like a game of Snakes and Ladders. Choices take us around the board, where we might slide down one of the snakes or climb a ladder. Progress is never smooth. The choices that come our way, the opportunities we encounter and how we deal with them, will make a big difference to our experience of that journey.

Networking offers many intersections. Online we may meet and converse with people from all over the world. Face-to-face we meet with people who are local to where we are at the time. Combine the two and you could be meeting locally with friends of your friends anywhere in the world.

While our personal journeys take us from birth to death, those are the only two certainties. It's what we do with the bit in the middle that makes a real difference. We should enjoy the journey while, if we choose to do so, leaving something behind for those who follow. As Robert Louis Stevenson said, "it is better to travel hopefully, than to arrive." The point of the journey is, perhaps, remaining fully alive, solvent and fulfilled until death arrives.

A Time of Change

Business is organising on a global scale, leading to a far more flexible approach to where and how things get done. Companies now think in terms of their core and non-core activities and the trend seems to be to do more with less employees.

People are expensive while software is cheap, therefore companies are electing to use software to avoid the need to spend money on people. In a Forbes.com article, *Ten Laws of the Modern World*, in April 2005, Rich Karlgaard quotes Gilder's Law (named for futurist George Gilder): "The best business models waste the era's cheapest resources in order to conserve the era's most expensive resources". Karlgaard comments, "Today the cheapest resources are computer power and bandwidth. Both are getting cheaper by the year (at the pace of Moore's Law). Google is a successful business because it wastes computer power – it has some 120,000 servers powering its search engine – while it conserves its dearest resource, people. Google has fewer than 3,500 employees, yet it generates $5 billion in (current run rate) sales."

More and more of the non-core work is being outsourced and significant amounts of this is being offshored.

At the same time, more people are choosing to downshift and work on areas that attract them, and that allow them to be passionate about what they do. They are choosing to balance their work and leisure time and improve their quality of life. This is leading to the growth of a self-employed class of professionals that Richard Duvall of Zopa, an Internet exchange for lenders and borrowers, referred to as "freeformers".

This view of our present – and our future – is supported in research by ethnographic researcher Bruce Davis. From his recent research,

Davis notes that our ways of earning money have changed and that we have become "more fluid and complex" in our needs of and uses for money. Our values are changing too. 2004 research 'Changing Lives', conducted by nVision and Taylor, Nelson, Sofres, noted that 54% of social groups A and B (professional and middle management) now want fulfilment above wealth and property.

In their background paper on 'freeforming', Zopa note that "Radical freeformers feel the disconnection most keenly. Many have sacrificed a measurable security of a monthly wage for intangibles like satisfaction, greater control, self-expression and time at home with a family. Freelancing, portfolio working, part-time work and job shares, home working and flexible hours are more and more commonplace – less than 50% of the working population have traditional full-time jobs today."

"People are fundamentally unhappy in their jobs," says Simon Woodroffe, founder of Yo! Sushi and a growing family of other Yo! businesses. "In surveys, people put job satisfaction down at number 10 on the list of things they get from their work and that's why an entrepreneurial society is erupting in Britain. More and more people dream of going out on their own. Everyone's got an idea for a business they could start."

A survey of 5900 managers for the Chartered Management Institute in the UK finds that a third do not take their full holiday entitlement. Patience Wheatcroft in the Times in July, 2005, reported that when they do take their full entitlement, they spend an average of an extra full day's work at the beginning and the end, just to manage a week off. "Sensible folk might bounce emails and telephone calls back to sender," she comments. "As it is, half of those taking holidays insist on phoning in while they're away whether their colleagues want them to or not. Half check their work e-mails, two in five check voice mails and 20% take their lap-tops".

A survey undertaken by Ecademy in association with Microsoft of over 700 members of the online Social Business Network underlined the results of that survey. 57% of respondents agreed that they 'work when away on holiday', with a quarter working more than one hour each day. Most common activities were checking email, checking voicemail, calling clients or customers, writing documents and calling colleagues. Chief Executive of Ecademy, Glenn Watkins comments, "In our survey, the key reasons people gave for working on holiday were the inability of others to cover their role and a worry that something will go wrong while they are away. While these ostensibly point to the failings of others, in reality they point to a lack of pre-holiday planning and the mistrust of colleagues on the part of the employees themselves. If people are going to get the break they deserve, they must take responsibility for making it happen." Having a trusted network of work colleagues would seem to be crucial here in reducing stress and allowing the employee to take their break free of work pressures.

Financial Crisis

As those older workers either choose to join the self-employed or find themselves unable to work for anyone else, the pensions systems that were so important to the choice of career for so many people are beginning to break down across the world. Fewer people are being born and we are living longer – a combination that means that many of us will have to work longer.

Not so long ago, it was possible to retire – sometimes as young as 50 – and live off an index-linked, final salary pension. Retirees in the last decades of the 20th century certainly had that possibility. That is no longer a possibility for many – maybe most – of us.

One group of people for whom that is still possible, as Patience Wheatcroft, business editor of The Times points out in her column 'Poor Old Public Sector? Give us a break' (The Times, 15th July, 2005), is the ever growing public sector in the UK (up by 270,000 jobs in 2002-4) most of whom "are still scheduled to retire at 60 on guaranteed salary related pensions."

More of us than ever now work for ourselves. Self-employment has always been a less dependable way of earning a consistent income and, as a result, many self-employed people find it difficult to save for their retirement. As more work is outsourced and offshored and as their numbers are swelled by the self-unemployed, it will become more difficult for self-employed people to earn and save sufficiently to be able to retire. As more people enter the market, so supply will drive down the fee value that can be earned in many areas. It may be balanced by increasing demand, though not necessarily in the same areas as there is supply, creating a need for retraining and cross skilling.

Add to that the pension crisis that is still unravelling globally, and we have a recipe for real problems. In an article 'The Demographic Shape of Things to Come' (Global Agenda Magazine) written in 2004, Adair Turner (now Baron Turner of Ecchinswell), Head of the UK Pensions Commission warned that "the world is relentlessly getting older with good and bad consequences." Traditionally, it has been those of working age who pay the pensions of the retired. For 20th century pensions "the relationship of contribution levels to benefit levels was only sustainable on the assumption that each generation was larger than the one before". The ratio between those aged 20 – 64 and those 65 or over is falling worldwide – the result of better healthcare and falling birth-rates, he notes – and that puts pensions at risk.

Demographics are changing across the world. Despite the AIDS epidemic in some parts of the world, life expectancy at birth and at 65 is increasing relentlessly in all successful economies, as noted by Turner in the 2004 article for Global Agenda. People are living around 1 1/2 years longer in every decade. The average age on Ecademy in 2005 is 46. It will not be uncommon to live to 90 by 2050, assuming that research continues to deliver cures for the illnesses of old age and that the economy does not implode in the interim.

Adair Turner comments that, at the same time, birth rates are falling to or below replacement levels. Against a replacement level of 2.05 children per woman in Western nations, many successful nations struggle to keep stability. Italy and Spain have 1.2 births per woman and France and Iceland have 1.89 and 1.95 respectively. The US has a birth rate of 2.05, but that is predicted to fall as birthrates among people of Hispanic origin fall. Turner likens the demographic shape to a column with a small pyramid on top, with each generation the same size as the one before and most people living to at least 60 or so, before dying over the next 30 to 40 years. As the lower part of the column narrows, the ratio of 20 – 64 year-olds to retirees will plummet. For example, Italy's ratio of 3.4 will drop to 1.4 by 2050, South Korea's from 9.0 to 1.7, Britain's from 3.7 to 2.1 and Iran's from 10.5 to 3.4.

Both longevity and birth rates "challenge existing pension systems", with a fall in fertility being a far more difficult issue. Turner notes: "In any pension system, the retirees who consume but do not produce, depend on the transfer of resources from the workers who produce, sacrificing or deferring some consumption by either taxes or savings."

If the current workers see no benefit in deferring consumption, it is the retirees who will feel the effects.

Many companies in the UK have already closed their final salary (defined benefit) pension schemes to new members. In December, 2005, Rentokil closed their final salary scheme altogether. A report published in October, 2004 by the UK Pensions Commission suggests that those that still exist could suffer a major shortfall. A shift to defined contribution schemes that depend on investments to purchase a pension on retirement and a trend to lower employer contributions could lead to a potential gap between savings and pension needs of £30 – £60 billion in the UK (Sunday Times, 22/5/05).

A report published in June, 2005 by the Association of Consulting Actuaries suggested that there may be a collective £130 billion funding shortfall among UK final salary pension schemes. In fact, nearly 9 out of 10 schemes now have a funding shortfall. To put this figure into perspective, there are only £131.2 billion of assets in all UK pension schemes (including defined contribution plans and group personal pensions).

Quoted in the Sunday Times in May 2005, Turner notes "We are clear that there is not a coherent long-term pensions system. It is agreed that the state ought to make sure by some means that everybody is out of poverty in retirement. The problem is there's not enough money. Remember, underlying this there is no free lunch. There are more people living longer and (that)... means there are some tricky choices about sums of money." Turner said, "I can't go through the figures at the moment, the numbers don't add up which is why you need some extra (national insurance) contributions."

In November, 2005, The Pensions Commission published its Second Report. Introducing the report Lord Turner said "It is wrong to talk about a crisis of pensioner income today, but the problems in the UK's pension system will grow increasingly worse unless a new pensions settlement for the 21st century is now debated, agreed and put in place". The report makes a number of recommendations including a National Pension Savings Scheme and a rise in State Pension Age by stages to 68 by 2050.

Despite initial press reports suggesting that UK Chancellor of the Exchequer, Gordon Brown, would decline to action the report on the grounds that some of its recommendations are 'unaffordable', these were subsequently denied. The report was welcomed by Alan Johnson, Secretary of State for Work and Pensions, who commented "This report brings home the message the Government first highlighted in the 2002 Green Paper; that people must either save more or work longer. In particular the analysis shows that occupational pension contributions and membership has been steadily slipping over at least two decades. These pressures have been largely unnoticed due to stock market exuberance." Time will tell whether the report's recommendations will be taken up. In the short term, the Commission suggests that employees and the self-employed should take responsibility for their own retirement funding.

It is highly unlikely that the Governments of the industrialised nations will be able to wave a magic wand to solve this problem. Both the US and the UK are reported to have massive debt problems that could also come back and bite them.

In the UK, reports Yahoo finance (analysis by Skipton Building Society) the next 10 years will see the debt mountain grow to £1.6 trillion from the current £1 trillion. That works out at an extra £600 billion or another £60 billion every year which is around £1000 for every man, woman and child in the UK. The society fondly hopes that it will mean a revival of saving as consumers attempt to plug the gaps in under-funded pensions. It also predicts we will have to work longer so we can afford to service our debts. But Skipton's Jennifer Holloway concludes we've gone from a culture of thrift to a culture of spend, and now to a culture of debt. We are a nation hooked on credit, and while for some of us it is a healthy obsession, for others it is dangerous and literally very costly.

Terence Samuel for CBS News reports that the US in early 2005 was $7,782,816,546,352 in debt in an economy worth $13 trillion. "Regardless of how it is sliced and diced, we are looking at an annual deficit of $368 billion this year and a 10-year projected deficit on $1.35 trillion, according to the Congressional budget office. And none of these numbers includes the cost of the continuing military operations in Iraq and Afghanistan. The President's suggestion in Parkersburg, that the $1.7 trillion in Treasury bonds held by the Social Security Administration is "not a pot of money to be drawn on" is a scary proposition. It not only threatens the future of social security, but he also goes to the heart of the debate over the long-term health and viability of the national economy. Debt and deficits, colliding with the spiralling costs of entitlements – Social Security, Medicare, Medicaid, farm subsidies, student loan programs – may mean that we are headed for desolate economic shoals". Newsweek's Robert Samuelson envisions it as an "economic and political death spiral".

Samuel goes on to note that the Comptroller General of the

General Accounting Office, David Walker, has been saying the solvency problem in Social Security is essentially a small stream headed for a much bigger river. "First, Social Security's financial challenge is a subset of our nation's financial and fiscal challenge," Walker told the House tax panel recently. "Social Security has an estimated under-funded commitment in current dollar terms for the next 75 years of $3.7 trillion. That compares with a roughly $43 trillion problem for our country. So the problem is not just that Social Security may not be able to mail out monthly cheques someday in the distant future but that it is, more perilously, that the Federal government may find itself so mired in debt that the whole economy just slowly grinds to a halt".

In contrast to the debt of some Western nations, India and China have cash. If they spend their cash in North America and Europe that is fantastic for us and they may well continue to consume our offices and golf courses and other facilities for a while, because it gives some status.

As lower level work migrates to lower cost economies, the developed nations need to consider providing value added services at the very top of the supply chain. That is they need to provide opportunities for self actualisation of those – in the old and new worlds – who have the money to afford it. We are talking here of manufacturing experiences rather than products. We need to manufacture an experience (see *The Experience Economy* by Joseph Pines) that people will want to consume and then leverage the value through our networks. Once a manufactured experience exists it needs to be exportable, because the money to buy it must flow from the places where the money exists. Trying to pull more money out of the already depleted service economy will not be a winning strategy.

Self Employed Networks (SENs)

With these changes to our working lives, come new solutions and adapted forms of working. We will work for more employers and for shorter periods, and some of us will alternate between operating as entrepreneurs and as employees.

Anita Campbell in a blog called 'Small Business Trends' notes, "the trend I am seeing increasingly is what I dubbed the 'on-again off-again entrepreneur.' The on-again off-again entrepreneur is someone who moves back and forth between being employed and owning his or her own business, multiple times. It's not an either or question: either being an entrepreneur your whole life, or being employed your whole life. More frequently these days, people are doing both at various times, moving in and out of entrepreneurship as the exigencies of earning a living force their hands".

Self-Employed Networks (SENs) will consist of a small core team of key workers and a pool of freelance workers who can be called upon for work. Some members of the network will need to become entrepreneurs and build the teams of people that they need to meet a particular project's needs. The core role of a SEN will be matching the efforts of the sales team with the availability and skills of the labour pool. They will also provide a communication channel that allows the network members to build relationships with their peer group. The model may be most reminiscent of the movie business, where teams of independent workers and small firms come together – often in a company specific to a single film – and work together towards a set of well-defined outcomes. At the end of the process, they go their separate ways to other projects, or to look for the next opportunity. We contend that many corporates will follow this route and have a core team with bought-in expertise providing further support as it is needed. Freeformers will bid their labour like an auction and project owners will bid for the best actors.

Charles Handy in his 1994 book 'The Empty Raincoat' referred to it as the Doughnut Principle – with his doughnut having a solid centre 'surrounded by hole'. "Much of life now looks like that doughnut. Organisations as well as individuals have come to realise that they have their essential core, a core of necessary jobs and necessary people, a core that is surrounded by an open and flexible space which they fill with flexible workers and flexible supply contracts." The Coase Theorem (see below) makes this doughnut approach more likely and more sustainable as transaction costs reduce towards zero.

For many of us, retirement will not be an option at all. There is no guarantee of, or indeed desire for, state support for those affected by changes to our working lives. So here is where a social support network will come into its own helping people with coping, finding work and earning and balancing their work with other activities.

There is a wealth of experience in the grey heads and, as the numbers of older people will continue to grow relative to the younger age groups, so older workers should find that their expertise and their labour comes back into demand.

A number of initiatives already exist. The Silver Fox Network, set up by Dr Gerry Lemberg and Ian Coburn, aims to capitalise on the skills and experience of older workers in supporting new enterprise. Mike Burnage is setting up the Wisdom Bank to match 'wisdom givers' with 'wisdom seekers' after realising that "retiring at 65 without an interest could cut your life short". Jim Tuffin of Biztime is encouraging the 'near retired' to network with those who can make use of their skills and experience – perhaps for money and perhaps purely for participation and involvement. (More about Global Labour Matching in Chapter 7.)

It has been said that search is the 'killer app' on the Internet, but search without finding is of little use to most of us. The main successes of the Internet era – Google, Yahoo, eBay and Amazon – are all matching engines. Google and Yahoo match you to information you need, eBay matches buyers and sellers, and Amazon matches you to books and, increasingly, to a wide range of consumer goods.

In the freeform world, freelance workers will need to be matched to suitable work. Unlike traditional recruitment, the need for a quick and accurate match will be paramount. Project owners will need to find whole teams or specific skilled individuals. Individuals will be looking for a continuity of work that fits their lifestyle AND their need for fulfilment. Social business networks will need to become the matching engines of the freeform generation. They should provide project owners with the ability to define opportunities and freelance workers with the ability to specify their needs and skill sets. Then the network can match their requirements and send offers to the freelancers that they may choose to take up. It's a buyer's and seller's market, and it is often as hard to buy (that is to find a scarce resource) as it is to sell.

The day will come, Thomas Power suggests, when you can log on to LinkedIn, openBC or Ecademy and there, in your inbox, will be the offers of work that you need for the next three to six months. Thomas sees that his job "is not to have a pretty website and offline events with Chardonnay but to put work on every member's table internationally". People join Ecademy to find work, and our job is to find that work and match them to it in an instant. Delivering on that need becomes a key part of Ecademy's mission. "We're not there yet," notes Thomas, "but we have to be as soon as we can."

In his 2005 book, *Winning by Sharing*, Léon Benjamin, adviser to Ecademy suggests that the future of work will continue the trend towards freelancing and portfolio working until "eventually most people will be portfolio workers; companies will be able to source people on demand, globally and virtually and the transition will be difficult but will bring about disproportionate rewards. The support economy has arrived to serve 21st-century portfolio workers."

For those who can adapt to this changed world – a world that offers fewer certainties and requires them to be responsible for maintaining both their skills and their marketing to a significant level – the overall effect will be more balanced. For those who cannot adapt, the consequences may be profound. With fewer safety nets, some people may not be able to survive. We may, indeed, be seeing a Darwinian change beginning, where those who can't adapt will be selected out of future generations. With fewer economic resources, will already-reducing populations continue that trend?

Wealth, noun (Shorter Oxford English Dictionary) –

1. The condition of being happy and prosperous; well-being (1652)

2. Prosperity consisting in abundance of possessions; riches; affluence (1645)

3. Economics. A collective term for those things the abundant possession of which constitutes riches, or 'wealth' in the popular sense (1821)

4. Plenty, abundance, profusion (of what is specified) (1596)

Most people use the word wealth to mean access to money, riches, property (shorter OED definitions 2 and 3 above). But is financial wealth alone, enough to sustain us throughout our journey? How does wealth as a wider concept help us in our journey?

Wealth is more than pure finance. Mother Teresa, for example, had no monetary wealth. She lived a life of deliberate poverty to meet her needs for great spiritual wealth – to meet her God in her purity – and helped thousands of people on the streets of India to spread emotional wealth.

John Peel, radio presenter and promoter of new music, lived Emotional Wealth thoughout his career. Peter Hook, bassist of band *New Order,* commented in a radio interview on the first anniversary of Peel's death, "We owe him a great deal and it's unrepayable, really. When we were nothing, he gave us a chance, for no financial reward, just the happiness of loving music".

A number of commentators talk about three types of wealth – material (financial), spiritual and emotional – and the need to balance them so that no one wealth becomes paramount. Abraham Maslow, in his hierarchy of needs, recognises that physical and survival needs – food, shelter, warmth – need satisfying first but suggests that as we satisfy those we move up a hierarchy at the top of which is self actualisation – being the best we can. The concepts that follow have as their assumption that basic needs have been satisfied.

Financial Wealth

We would generally accept that financial wealth is about money and resources that convert readily to money, such as property. Acquiring money and goods is a target for many people on their individual journeys, and this book will not suggest that this aim is wrong. Becoming rich and earning rewards for your labour are values we espouse. However, we contend that financial wealth alone is unbalanced and will lead to a less than fulfilling life in the longer term.

Money is important in making sure that the planet has resources to grow and develop — it is most powerful when it moves around. Roger Hamilton, Chairman of XL Group (see Wealth Dynamics, Chapter 13), contends that money is like a river. It should be flowing and it only flows from higher ground to lower ground. So the height of the source of a river is one factor in its existence. Another factor is the amount of water available at the source. Whilst water is flowing in, the river will form itself and find its path to the sea. When it dries up and no water flows, the river continues to exist and as soon as water returns it will flow again.

So, says Hamilton, it is with wealth. The higher the value differential we create, the bigger the slope it creates. As soon as money flows, it follows the path from high to low value. If it dries up, the wealth is still there and money will be able to flow again. In other words, wealth is what you have left when all the money has gone. It is why some people create many successful businesses in their lives and, even when they fail, they can return and rebuild. We will talk about the components of wealth in Hamilton's view in a later section.

So, if financial wealth can dry up, what prevents us from simply shrivelling up and dying when it does? We have emotional and spiritual wealth to sit back on. We'll talk about spiritual wealth first as emotional wealth is a major component of Ecademy's philosophy and will need more time and more detailed treatment.

Spiritual Wealth

Spiritual wealth is focused on us and how we process the ups and downs of life. We talk about people 'having spirit' or giving 'spirited performances'. It is our personal drive. Some people depend upon religion to a greater or lesser extent to provide their spiritual input. All religions offer the opportunity for meditation or prayer and provide teachings that seek to set norms of behaviour and belief. Recent generations in some Western countries have shunned religion or moved it down their priorities, while seeking other spiritual experiences. These may be physical or mental activities and are often a combination of both. The simple act of walking in a beautiful place has both physical and mental effects. Some of our most spectacular environments take us into literally new territory – we are awed and uplifted by it. From our spiritual wealth we can develop a path and a set of values that will guide us when we need to make adjustments to our life.

Emotional Wealth

Some of you may be asking, "What have emotions got to do with business?" You won't be alone. In the business world it has been common to think this way. To consider that business is (or should be) somehow devoid of human feeling. For very many participants, that approach leads to emotions and hurts being internalised and carried either into the home and non-working life of the individual or towards an inevitable breakdown. We contend that a healthy acceptance of the emotional nature of ourselves and of others can lead to a better, richer business experience.

Emotional wealth is outward facing. It is how you decide to be perceived in the outside world by anyone from close family to total strangers. It emanates partly from the conscious mind and partly from your subconscious, where it reflects your spiritual wealth or poverty. Tobin Smith, a writer on financial wealth and investment comments, "I have learned one simple and immutable truth over the last 30 or so years; success in life is of course NOT measured by the quality and amount of financial assets that we acquire, but in the quality and amount of emotional assets – the people, passions and rewarding experiences that we acquire - that brings joy that adds genuine value to life." Sam Lim adds, "Emotional Wealth is really about acquiring positive traits associated with personal success. Positive attitude, self discipline and wisdom are some of the emotional wealth that we should aspire to have."

Smith sees the measurement of emotional wealth in the same way as financial wealth. There is a bank account and an asset register for emotional wealth. In his blog 'Revisiting Emotional Wealth Building 101' he goes on to say "I can tell you that if you do not actively manage your emotional asset portfolio, it will wither away and FAIL to pay enough emotional dividends to exceed your emotional expenses."

Penny Power sees emotional wealth as the give in relationships, whilst financial wealth is what you receive as a result. Emotional wealth "is the part that gives you a real high and reflects who you are. It is the part that builds the relationship with others using transparency, honesty and genuine interest in making the connec-tion. Financial wealth is the outcome of emotional wealth i.e. it is the result and the ability to receive what someone wants to give to you." It is a natural environment that you create that makes others want to give to you. (See pages 42 to 45 for more).

Just as with a bank account, deposits have to be made, usually before withdrawals can happen. To give before trying to receive makes logical sense. To give without even a thought of what may come back makes emotional sense. It is the principle of paying forward – helping someone else – rather than paying back. If we all pay forward, someone's gives will become your receipts and it is important to receive them gratefully and gracefully. Your giving nature will be noticed by others and it will attract people and luck towards you.

Do we get Emotional Wealth from online transactions? Could we? We buy things from Amazon and eBay and find things using Google and Yahoo. But do any of them actually deliver any emotional wealth. The transactions themselves don't appear to have any emotion attached to them, but the goods that are bought do. One of the problems with all of the four web sites is actually getting hold of people rather than the robotic front-end on the Web. It is this that possibly precludes them from delivering emotional wealth. When there is interaction with people, it is different. Amazon, for example, provides you with a literate friend – other customers just like you – who you can consult on the Internet, so maybe there is emotional wealth in that. Emotional wealth comes from a connection with people and with their passion.

In the delivery of higher value or critical services there is probably more need for the emotional side as well. If you are looking to buy something that you may only buy once in a lifetime, then word-of-mouth referral from someone that you already trust, and on whose word you can depend, will help you find the right person to do the work. What will also help is if that person attests as to the reliability and the friendliness and the ability to do business with that person. That they are an easy person to get along with may also be important.

Social and Business networks provide the opportunity for inter-actions of this nature with people. It is in the connections made online that Emotional Wealth can be delivered and built.

Emotional Wealth – *Connecting your heart to your head*
Blog by Penny Power – October 18th, 2005

> *You know the moment when you meet someone and you feel they can make a difference in your life? This is Emotional Wealth.*
>
> *Through my business life, I have met many people who commun-icate at a higher level. Finding out what this is, has been my passion since I started Ecademy. What is it that makes some business people more attractive to know than others? Why are they more successful, when they do not seem driven or ambitious, they are just great to know? But, how come, almost despite themselves, they are very successful, and they appear to "have it all"? Their network supports them and they have true Network Value.*
>
> *My desire to understand this and be able to articulate this to others has been a purpose for me for 3 years. My hope that I can teach this to Ecademy Members and help them to be more successful is what drives me.*
>
> *Our vision for Ecademy is to 'Connect business people, to learn, network and develop their emotional and financial wealth.' I now know that by becoming driven by their emotional wealth, this gives them purpose for themselves and their business, but fundamentally, it will change the world into a less angry, less greedy place to be.*
>
> *I would like to stress that Emotional Wealth is not about giving all your money away. It does not mean you need to work for free. It does not mean you need to de-focus from your business. It means finding the purpose within yourself that is reflected through the skills you have, providing you with the words and delivery that makes a difference to others.*

Let's take the example of an Accountant. He is 45 years old, he is bringing in enough money for his family, he is skilled and he is respected. But, he is bored, he lacks purpose and work has become a means to an end. This feeling will exude from him. His clients, his colleagues, his friends and most importantly his family will feel this. But why is he an accountant?

When he was a little boy, he loved numbers, he was top of the class, and numbers were a game to him. As he grew up he just knew that numbers were his talent, numbers were his passion and he definitely wanted to work with numbers. In fact he knew he could make a difference to others with numbers. So he became an Accountant. A successful Accountant. But now at 45, he wonders what it is all about. Each day he gets up. He has meetings with clients, checks spreadsheets and gives advice. The day ends, he comes home, exhausted and then repeats the whole thing all over again. The passion, the purpose is missing. He is emotionally dead in business.

You ask him why he does it and he replies 'it pays well' or 'it is all I know'. He is actually living the life that he wanted but the purpose is not there, he's lost the passion for what he does. This does not mean he needs to change direction, this does not mean he is having a mid-life crisis, what he needs is an injection of Emotional Wealth.

I said earlier that Emotional Wealth makes you more attractive to know. This, once found and communicated, provides purpose and drive. It changes the way people feel about you. I am going to come back to our Accountant later. Save the thought.

We have all been taught to talk about our products and services as features and benefits. Emotional Wealth is the next layer, and it is the most important one.

The world is competitive, there are no shortages of skills, there are directories online and offline that can help you find what you need. Business cards are given out like sweeties, and they are forgotten and left to rot by those you give them to. The next phase is online networking.

But what is online networking?

Is it yet another contact directory? Another place to collect skills and names? Or, is it somewhere where you can create network value, have others talk about you when you are not with them. Your network refers people to you, because they know you 'can make a difference'.

I believe that it is the second. It is relationship building. It is creating long-lasting relationships that are built on trust, and it is about creating the value in your network that tells others "I can make a difference".

Let's go back to our Accountant. He is now sitting in front of a client and he wants to win their business. Why? Because this is what his life needs, this is what he 'does'. But, instead of talking about his business, his skills and his price, he says this, "Do you know, I love numbers. Numbers have been my passion since I was a little boy. I am living a life I dreamed of. I work with numbers. I was always top of my class and I can read numbers like you read stories or poems. They talk to me. The talent I had as a little boy has now grown into a strong skill. My passion is to use this skill to save your business money. My purpose in life is to make a difference to others by using this talent and I will do this with more passion than you have ever experienced from an Accountant".

To have Emotional Wealth you need to know the difference you make to others, know the Emotional Wealth Value that you have. You have been on a journey though life, and you are now living the life you were destined for, but do you know this yet, have you connected your heart to your head? Do you know how to connect your heart to someone else's.

Hearts have an infinite amount of space, unlike heads, which *are over-loaded and over-stimulated. Connecting your heart to someone else's will establish you as the person who makes a difference to others, your network will remember you, you will be lodged in their heart. This is the new world, this is how we will all progress and make the world a better place. Once you have identified your Emotional Wealth, you will know the part you have in its progress, and in the lives of others.*

The Internet is Matching

With the growth and spread of the Internet and the increases in bandwidth both within the network and for internet users, it has begun to be part of many people's daily life. Whilst there is still a 'digital divide', the spread of the Internet to the less developed part of the globe has allowed them to compete on a more level platform. Almost 1 billion people now (November 2005) have access to the Internet, according to www.internetworldstats.com, representing 15.2% of the world's 6.4 billion population. Greatest penetration is in the USA (68.2% of population) followed by Australia/Oceania (52.9%) and Europe (35.5%). Africa with 2.7%, the Middle East (8.6%) and Asia with 9.2% have the least proportion of their populations online. Asia has over half of the world's population and internet usage in that region is likely to grow. As Thomas Friedmann argues in the FT Book of the Year, 2005 'The World is Flat' the availability of the Internet and of increasingly powerful tools to leverage its power, have made it easier to get started in many businesses and made it easier to trade globally. The Internet is bringing down the barriers to trade across the globe.

As the World Wide Web and its associated tools become more available, it is tempting to believe that the Internet is simply about improving and increasing the content that is found there. To use a simple analogy, that puts the Web into the same category as a newspaper, except with billions of pages and widely differing reliability of the information found there. Maybe content is not the only important element in the success of the Internet.

In an article from *First Monday* titled *Content is not King*, Andrew Odlyzko argues that the Internet is primarily regarded as a content delivery system. Yet, historically, connectivity has mattered much more than content. Even on the Internet, content is not as important as is often claimed, since it is the connectivity of e-mail that drives most people to first get connected. However, the current growth of blogging and social and business networks suggests that connectivity matched with content is what most users are seeking. Blogs can be instant two-way conversations – though many are not.

The Online Publishers Association (www.online-publishers.org) publish an Internet Activity Index that "provides a new way of looking at consumer engagement online, dividing Internet Usage into four distinct activities: content, communications, commerce and search." Their November 2005 statistics for share of time show communications at 41.5% of time, content at 35%, commerce at 18.7% and search at 4.8%.

In the first wave of major Internet successes, content has been important, as has the ability of the user to engage with it. As we have already noted, Google, Yahoo, eBay and Amazon are all matching engines.

Skype provides communication matching for a growing body of Voice over IP (VoIP) users and is being integrated with eBay, who acquired them in September, 2005 for approximately $2.6 billion in cash and eBay stock, and networking services globally. Skype claim there have been over 150m downloads of their software and that they have 3m people online at any one time. Over 100,000 people in a month paid €20 for Skypeout – a service that allows users to make calls to any number from their Skype system at favourable rates.

The Big Internet players are not yet big players when compared with established companies. The two founded in 1994 had turnovers for the first three quarters of 2005 of $3.7 billion (est $5bn for full year) (Yahoo) and $5.5 billion (full year estimate $8bn) (Amazon). Ebay, founded September 1995, turned over $3.2 billion for the same period (full year estimate 4.3bn). Google, the baby of the four and founded in 1998, weighs in at $4.2 Billion ($6bn full year est). Their estimated aggregate turnover of $23 billion may just place them into the Fortune 100. After 10 years and around $500 billion of venture capital, the four top players represent less in turnover terms than British Telecom and are approaching a third of the UK's largest retailer, Tesco. The world's largest retailer – WalMart – had a turnover of more than $285 billion in 2005.

In 1975 a small company called Microsoft was started. The company floated in 1986 with revenues of $50 million. In the 10 years of the Big four on the Internet, they have grown to be much bigger than Microsoft was at that age. Microsoft has since gone on to grow by 800 times in 19 years – reporting turnover of just below $40 billion in 2005. For all of the Big four to achieve a similar growth pattern for the next 19 years is highly unlikely, but if the ultimate winners of the Internet matching market had a combined income of, say, 800 times that of Google today, that market would be worth $4,800 billion. On this basis, the market capitalisation of the eventual victor could be as much as $60 trillion. Ridiculous of course, but it shows the potential for growth, even if it is less than this highly suspect number. Many factors will arise to affect that growth, and many companies in non-Internet markets will be involved in the consolidation that might produce such a market. The real potential of the Internet is as yet untapped.

On the matching front, UK company Zopa has created an exchange where private lenders can match with borrowers to create a matching exchange that has a personal touch. It is aimed at those people – and they are many – who would prefer not to do business with the banking sector. How long before insurance and mortgages move this way?

One of the phenomena of the Internet has been the effect it has on what is offered. With the digitisation of product such as music, books, images and software, and the means to deliver it economically, it has been possible to offer ever-greater ranges of product to a market that will seemingly consume them, without significant additional operational costs to the retailer. In his article on 'The Long Tail' in Wired magazine, Chris Anderson takes the example of the book market. An average Barnes and Noble (in the US) carries 130,000 titles, he says. "Yet more than half of Amazon's book sales come from outside its top 130,000 titles. Consider the implication: if the Amazon statistics are any guide, the market for books that are not even sold in the average bookstore is larger than the market of those that are. In other words the potential book market may be twice as big as it appears to be, if only we can get over the economics of scarcity." Anderson notes that people are going deep into the catalogue in a number of sectors, down a long list of available titles that is way beyond what is available at Blockbuster Video, Tower Records, and Barnes and Noble. "And the more they find, the more they like".

Key to Anderson's thesis is the change that the Internet has made to the amount of space available. Not just the Internet, of course, with Satellite and Cable TV offering hundreds, maybe thousands of channels to service the long tail. When space was restricted, we took our choices from those made available to us by the record companies, TV stations and retail buyers. Now it is not, the demand is coming from the bottom up – from the consumer – and the market is able to respond to their needs and wants because space (and bandwidth) is getting greater all the time.

Being able to offer a wide range of goods or services also depends on being able to create alliances and to find suppliers and affiliates quickly. Here, some of the early work of economist Ronald Coase is often cited. Coase, who was professor emeritus at the University of Chicago Law School during the dot com boom, wrote a paper in 1937 on The Nature of the Firm which was cited in 1991 when he was awarded a Nobel Prize for economics.

In a New York Times article, 'Coase's Ideas Flourish in the Internet Economy' in 2000, Bob Tedeschi noted the relevance of the Coase theory to the Internet age. Coase considered the factors in making a decision to produce a product or service internally or to outsource it. As well as market prices, he noted that there were significant transaction costs involved in finding a supplier and creating an agreement. Since Coase wrote his theory, in a time of prohibitively high transaction costs "transaction costs have plunged, thanks to the Internet. Within the so-called new economy, information itself is typically the product, and that information moves at the speed of a T1 (high speed leased) line. As a result, companies can get complete information about potential suppliers and business partners within a few clicks, and can therefore set up supplier agreements or form alliances with other companies for a fraction of what it would have cost even a decade ago".

Anderson uses as his example of the Long Tail, a provider of music called Rhapsody (www.rhapsody.com). He notes that as Rhapsody added tracks to their offer, the demand kept going. "Not only is every one of Rhapsody's top 100,000 tracks streamed at least once a month, the same is true for its top 200,000, top 300,000, and top 400,000. As fast as Rhapsody adds tracks to its library, those songs find an audience, even if it's just a few people a month somewhere in the country. This is the long tail." Rhapsody now lists over one million songs.

In the Wired article, Venture Capitalist and former music industry consultant Kevin Laws puts it this way: "The biggest money is in the smallest sales." Another way of looking at this phenomenon is that Internet companies need to deliver huge value for tiny money. They have to deliver 'disproportionate value'. For example, eBay now has 135 million customers which, according to a CNBC special on the company, would make them the ninth most populous nation in the world. This year alone, all those sellers will list 1.8 billion items for auction, which will exceed the 2004 figure of $40 billion of vendor sales on the platform. The sellers involved with the site might all correctly believe they had a hand in it.

eBay's offer to sellers is very relevant to the mood of the age. Instead of spending 40+ hours per week working for an employer, they can choose to work for themselves. Meg Whitman of eBay is prepared to offer corporate perks to self-employed people who sell substantial amounts through the network – known as Powersellers. For Titanium powersellers (turnover of $150,000 per month) these benefits can include healthcare solutions for the powerseller and their employees and training and development from eBay to help develop their business. This is a network offering self-employed people the perks of big company employment. Maybe networks will become the new corporates and corporates will become the new networks.

One consequence of the lower transaction costs associated with the Internet is that individuals can be much more engaged in the process of deciding and developing how the products and services with which they interact develop. Zopa quote a number of examples that also appear in the book 'Emergence' by Steven Johnson. eBay of course, is a classic case of development being driven, in part at least, by the users of the system. Linux, and the Open source movement of which it is a part, have developed because of the involvement and dedication of coders across the world in writing and testing modules of code which they then make freely available to the world. One of the fastest growing browsers currently, Firefox, developed by Mozilla Foundation, a Californian not-for-profit company, is entirely free to use and has been developed from the ground up since June 2003 by voluntary coders, with startup support from the AOL Netscape Division.

The creators of the Sims computer game released tools that allow players to design their own content for the game. Within a year, there were hundreds of independent content creators, and more than 200 fan websites offering other players over half a million collectable items. Now 90% of the game has been created by those enthusiasts. Charles Leadbeater and Paul Miller term them Pro-ams in the Pro-Am revolution (Demos 2004). "The Sims community is a distributed, bottom-up, self-organising body of pro-am knowledge, in which players are constantly training one another and innovating," they say.

In the study, Leadbeater and Miller quote Seb Potter, Pro-Am open source programmer, "For me work is the oddity. Work is a kind of compromise. I do work which is as close as possible to my passions to make working tolerable. But I feel most myself when I am doing this open source stuff. When I am doing this and give it my complete and full attention then everything else around me fades away and dissolves and I become completely focused".

So how will the matching needed for these changes develop? The basic models are developing already in social and business networks.

The Market

Networking is not new. Ever since Stone Age man hunted in packs, we have got together with others to share skills, experience, workload and to support each other. There have been guilds, unions, friendly societies as well as groups based around church, school and sports clubs. Brownies, Cubs, Scouts and Guides are all networks. We all have membership of several at any one time – including the one closest to home – our family.

For those whose path will take them into freelance work or self-employment, the model employed by those Stone Age men, is one that will be readily recognised. For most sole traders, the need to find people to surround them is paramount. Business needs to be found and won. In most cases, hunting for business in packs will improve your chances of success immensely. Networks provide the raw material for the development of teams across skill sets, and with online networks, that can be done across the world.

Offline Networks

Until relatively recently, most networking took place in a room with all of the networkers physically present. That option still works well and many of the online networks also run physical meetings. Meeting face to face offers an opportunity to 'look the other person in the eyes' and to make an assessment of trustworthiness.

In business, Chambers of Commerce have provided face-to-face networking opportunities for many years. Even the Trade Unions have begun to provide networking and signposting for their members, recognising the changes in the way work is performed in the 21st-century. Through initiatives like Union Learning Representatives, they are working with management teams to encourage their members to study for qualifications and to better themselves as a result.

In the early 21st century you can network over Breakfast (BNI, BRE, Business over Breakfast), Lunch (NRG) and Dinner with networking groups providing opportunities to listen to speakers and to meet new people. 'We Entrepreneurs' offers networking without an agenda for "ambitious business owners with ambitious company growth plans and minimum turnover of £200,000 … to learn from each other in an open and trusted environment, to exchange ideas and information thus helping each other develop their businesses". Business Networking International (BNI) offers a form of networking called 'strong contact' where a group of people of different trades and professions come together every week for breakfast and pass each other referrals for business. We will discuss strong contact networking as contrasted with 'Strength of Weak Ties' later in this book.

Online Networks

In the early days of the Internet, making contact with other users depended upon the basic protocols. Files could be sent using File Transfer Protocol (FTP) and conversations could be set up using Telnet.

Later, Usenet and Listserv groups were developed, where many contributors could take part in 'threaded' conversations. It helped to be technically adept to use these facilities. Early Bulletin Board and conferencing systems like FIDO and CIX (Compulink Information Exchange) emerged during the 1980s. The interfaces between the personal computers of the day were still slow (typically 50 – 100 times slower than broadband) and quite difficult to use. CIX was picked up by the Times newspaper in the UK in the early 1990s through a conference moderated by the late – and much missed – John Diamond, making CIX one of the first conferencing systems to be used by less technical people. Andy Coote became part of the Internet revolution through Diamond's weekly column in The Times, *Enter Password* which summarised the online forum activity.

As the Web developed, a start-up company, 'e-groups', began to offer an online collaboration service. Messages could be added or read, files uploaded and pictures appended. e-groups quickly became a standard way for global project teams to share ideas. Yahoo bought e-groups in August 2000, when they were renamed Yahoo groups. They remain a simple way of setting up a collaborative group and many of the standards groups which were developing the Internet used private Yahoo groups for project team conversations and public groups for user education. Most Yahoo groups can be used simply by sending and receiving e-mail and, as such, tend not to be real-time or interactive.

Instant messaging filled the interactive gap, initially for home users, but it is increasingly being used by business people for key conversations in real-time. Voice over IP services like Skype now offer instant messaging alongside free Internet calls.

Craigslist (www.Craigslist.com) offers a slightly tangential approach to social and business networks. Founded in 1995 by Craig Newmark, Craigslist is a set of hyperlinked lists to useful resources including 'small ads' posted by its members. It began in San Francisco and spread, city by city, to the major population centres of the US and to other parts of the world. It is mentioned here for two reasons

- Its policy of taking small ads for little or (mostly) no cost has been seen by some as a threat to the big media operators of local newspapers (see below)

- In August 2004 eBay bought a 25% stake in Craigslist (through a deal examined in more detail below) raising rumours that eBay might swallow Craigslist and accelerate the growth of small ads on eBay. To date, that has not happened and both eBay and Craigslist are making happy noises about synergy as separate operations.

In the late 1990s, a number of developers began trying to combine the best of Yahoo groups with more interactive facilities. The current crop of social and business networks mostly come from that wave of development and each, as we will see, has its own emphasis and mixture of features.

It can be argued that all online networks are to some extent social. They all allow individuals to find and connect with other individuals whether for dating, to discuss music or film, to do business or to develop affiliate and business partners. So with most networks, it is a matter of the owners' and the members' choice whether they become purely social, purely business or a mixture of social and business. As the tools are similar, it will be the membership that is attracted that will decide where the majority of activity sits. Business can and will be done on 'social' sites and social activity including dating – sometimes leading to marriage – will take place on 'business' sites.

So what are the tools of the social and business networks? All offer the facility to create a profile which may be minimalist or may become a home page for the individual. Being seen and understood is the first requirement of a profile and we deal more with that later in the book. A good profile and a professional photograph will attract the right people towards you and allow you to build a network.

Building a network, using the social and business networking platform, is another commonly-used tool provided by nearly all networks. To help with the building personal networks, some of the social and business networks also allow members to create and join clubs to discuss topics of common interest. Many networks offer the face-to-face approach as well with meetings organised by members. Meetup.com, backed by Pierre Omidyar of eBay, specialises in this area.

The problem of trust in an online environment will be explored further in a later section of this book. The social and business networks have taken different approaches to mitigating this problem. Some only allow connection through a trusted third party, e.g. LinkedIn, while others operate a form of reputation management. eBay and Amazon rate both buyers and sellers based on their activity and the feedback they get from other members. Ecademy has a simpler system of allowing members to rate each other 'good'. Most sites allow testimonials to be added to the profile of members, providing some third-party trust.

Another aspect of creating attractiveness, whether to other members, partners, funders or employers, is to create relevant and useful content. This can be in the form of blogs (weblogs) or articles. Some social business networks have the facility to allow comments on the content that members provide. We talk about good content creation and how it might make you more visible (for good or ill) later in the book.

Where Craigslist has come from classified advertising towards social networking, some of the other social and business networks have moved in the opposite direction and now offer member adverts on their sites. Ecademy now offers Blogging (associated with Emotional Wealth) and Flogging (selling through the Marketplace – about Financial Wealth) on the same page.

Increasingly, content placed in a blog or marketplace advertisement will be picked up and listed by services like Google Blogsearch and Google Base, as well as on the main search engines.

Monetising the Networks

In an article for CNET in June, 2005, Molly Wood sets out what she believes are the five problems with social networking. They are "there's nothing to do there"; "it takes too much time"; "traffic alone isn't enough"; "strangers kind of suck (or, put nicely, the social hierarchy is really not that attractive)" and "we already have the Internet". Sites that succeed will need to overcome these five objections. In other words, sites have to be interesting and useful to get traffic and even more so to get revenue.

Gary Rivlin in the New York Times in September 2005 reported that David Sze, a venture capitalist at Greylock Partners, was a sceptic of the millions of dollars being poured into Internet companies that were creating online communities to foster business and social contacts. "Basically, it reminded us a lot of what we saw in the late 1990s," Mr Sze said of the first rush of investment in social networking ventures in 2003. "It was, 'let's hope some users come and if they do, we'll figure out how to turn that into a business.' We didn't see a real business model there."

"Even now a year and a half later, the question persists of how these ventures can make money and justify the millions already invested." notes Rivlin. "Still, some of the start-ups have shown such impressive growth in number of users that they are starting to win backing from sceptics like Mr Sze. And there are some signs that selling classified ads on these websites may be a solid business model."

"A lot of these social network sites had built up a sizeable base of users due to the viral nature of how they operate," agrees Brad Bowers, a partner with BlackInc Ventures, a business development and merger and advisory firm focused on Internet companies quoted in a CNET news article. "However, as we learn from the dot-com boom, successful companies must find ways to monetise these users in order to build lasting, successful businesses".

OpenBC is already profitable in Germany. Ecademy trades profitably and is growing fast. Other networks will certainly follow.

Social Networks

Social networks, typically mass-market, are undergoing dramatic and far-reaching changes. The sector seems set for a major battle for control between the start-up networks and the bigger IT players, Yahoo, Google and Microsoft among them. News Corporation has recently entered the space with the $580 million acquisition of Intermix Media, owners of mySpace the most active social network of the moment. According to comScore Media Metrix, MySpace receives 14 million unique visitors a month compared to one million unique visitors to Friendster, its nearest rival.

The major players like Yahoo, MSN and Google, whose Orkut site is popular in South America, would seem best placed to divide up the market between them, but the arrival of News Corporation, whose record with new media investments must surely improve, adds a new dimension. The Rupert Murdoch led company has given considerable emphasis to the web in recent months. They held two web summits in six months in 2005 and appointed Jeremy Philips to the office of the Chairman as Executive Vice President focusing on acquisitions and strategy across the company and on Internet investments. As we discuss below, traditional media outlets are beginning to feel the pressure of a more Internet-centric world and may need to get involved to find a secure future. The decline in print news that 24-hour rolling television news has begun, could be compounded by social networking sites.

Friendster

Friendster, founded in 2003 by Jonathan Abrams, was, initially the lead player in the Social Networking space. It won several awards in the early days and still talks of having more than 16 million members. However, according to press reports, Friendster has been having a more difficult time during 2004/2005.

A New York Times article 'Friendster, Love and Money' by Gary Rivlin in January, 2005, notes that people were talking about Friendster for all the wrong reasons. "That is because the company, which endured three Chief Executives during 2004, has seen a spate of senior executives depart in recent weeks. Just as troubling, a younger, flashier rival called mySpace has eclipsed Friendster, at least in the United States, amongst those in the most highly coveted 18 to 29 demographic."

Friendster received roughly $13 million in venture funding in October 2003, most of it from Benchmark Capital and Kleiner Perkins Caufield and Byers. However, according to comScore Media Metrix, in March 2005, Friendster had 975,000 unique visitors down from a high of around 1.75 million unque visitors in October, 2003. By contrast, 11.3 million users visited MySpace in March, 2005 and 4.1 million people visited thefacebook.

The departure of Scott Sassa as CEO in mid 2005 and his replacement by Taek Kwon, formerly the executive vice president of product and technology at Citysearch.com, had media commentators and analysts speculating about the viability of not just Friendster but the whole Social Networking Sector. "I think Friendster really missed their big opportunity," said Mark J. Pincus, who is an investor in Friendster and the founder of Tribe networks, "They weren't quick to turn on new functionality, where a company like mySpace kept innovating and adding new features."

In an article in September, 2005, also in the New York Times, Rivlin notes that Friendster is cash-flow positive through the sale of ads on its site. "The looming question is whether it will earn the kind of revenues that venture capitalists need to see when investing $13 million in a single start-up."

MySpace

The largest and most active of the purely social networks in the online space is MySpace, with some 14 million unique visitors a month. It was recently, with its owner Intermix media, acquired by News Corporation for $580 million, the first move by "big media" into the networking space – but probably not the last. With venture capital of just $5 million from Redpoint ventures, MySpace has all the potential to be a successful model for Social Networking.

Steve Rosenbush in a May 2005 article 'Why MySpace is the Hot

Place' for Business Week comments "This 20-month-old social networking site has left pioneer Friendster way behind. Now it's looking to cash in on its ever-growing cachet. Thanks to its addictive appeal, MySpace has become one of the hottest properties on the Web."

Rosenbush goes on to note that "MySpace is based on a core of music fans. From the beginning of the site it catered to musicians. Bands can create their own home pages, with photos, tour dates, and as many as four songs – all for free. Marquee names like Beck, the Black Eyed Peas, and ex-Smashing Pumpkins leader Billy Corgan joined. That pulled in fans and their friends, who all found that MySpace offered loads of options that other sites lacked. Besides posting photos and personal information, users can add blogs, message boards, and music and video they made themselves."

MySpace is a site with a very young demographic. It is very 'Sex 'n' Drugs and Rock 'n' Roll' and the first and last of those are very evident from even a quick visit to the site. Compared to Friendster, it seems edgy and dangerous – good points for its target market. How it will change under new ownership and whether the demographic will relate well to their details being owned by such a major corporation will reveal in time. As this is written, MySpace dominates the market. The Independent in early January, 2006 reports that "Angry members of MySpace, the personal file-sharing website for young adults, are accusing Rupert Murdoch's News Corporation of censoring their postings and blocking their access to rival sites. The 38 million subscribers to MySpace, which News Corp bought for $629m (£355m) last July, discovered that when they wrote to each other about rival video-swapping site YouTube, the words were automatically deleted, and attempts to download video images from YouTube led to blank screens". "MySpace is supposed to be a personal forum!" wrote 'Makisha' at the blog site Supr.c.iliu.us. "Now it's owned by some corporation and it's being sensored [sic]! The beauty of it has been ruined. Better wise up MySpace or you're going to loose [sic] a good portion of your subscribers."

A spokesman for MySpace told the Independent that it would not explain how the blocking of YouTube came about, nor how it was resolved, nor whether in future it would continue to block links to rival websites or censor messages between MySpace customers.

orkut

According to its own website, "orkut is an online community website designed for friends. The main goal of our service is to make your social life, and that of your friends, more active and stimulating. orkut's social network can help you both maintain existing relationships and establish new ones by reaching out to people you've never met before. Who you interact with is entirely up to you. Before getting to know an orkut member, you can even see how they're connecting to you through the friends network."

Famously, membership of orkut is only available through the invitation of another member. The introduction goes on to mention many uses for the site including sharing hobbies and interests, looking for romantic connections or establishing new business contacts. Those are not the only uses of orkut if the BBC News Online site is to be believed.

In July 2005 the BBC site reported that "10 people have been arrested in Brazil after authorities discovered them allegedly using Google's online community site, orkut, to sell drugs. The drugs ring was uncovered after police tapped phone calls and monitored on-line communications through orkut. As the BBC noted, orkut is very popular in Latin America: "According to media reports, more than half of the 7 million community members are from Brazil."

In his blog on the BBC online on March 2004, Bill Thompson agonised over whether to join. "Orkut is already seen as the Groucho club of social networking sites, so joining could do even more damage to my credibility in the online world than arguing that Linux might conceivably contain some code that belongs to other people. It pretends to be exclusive, since you can only join by invitation. It is associated with Google, the mighty lord of search engines, so will eventually be bankrolled by millions of advertising dollars. And the website has the sort of mildly ironic postmodern self-deprecating style that we all associate with the worst sort of reverse snobbery and academic pretension. You almost expect to find Julie Burchill waiting at the virtual door." Time will tell if Google's bankroll will come out for orkut and whether that will be the only criterion for success.

Yahoo! 360°

Yahoo, which has 112 million registered users, has launched its social networking site called Yahoo! 360° which, in September 2005, is currently in Beta. The site offers a number of facilities tied into a Yahoo! ID. These include a personal Blog with the ability to send text and photos from your mobile phone to your blog, a shareable photo album, the ability to create lists of "books, music, movies, TV shows, and more", instant messaging (branded as "Blast") and a "LAUNCHcast Station" your own Yahoo! Music station.

First impressions suggest that it lacks the style and edge of MySpace but this may be overcome by the sheer marketing muscle of Yahoo.

MSN Spaces

Microsoft is a major player in the communication market through Hotmail for email and MSN for instant messaging. Business Week's Rosenbush notes that "MSN launched a similar site [to MySpace], dubbed Spaces, in April – and signed up 10 million users in a matter of weeks."

According to the Microsoft web site "MSN® Spaces is an entirely new free offering from MSN that allows consumers to create personal Internet Spaces, sites where they can express themselves in a variety of ways and interact with the people they care about most. MSN Spaces is more than an ordinary personal Web site; it's an easy-to-use service that is more like a dynamic online scrapbook, giving people a place to create and update a Web log, or blog, and share their photos, music playlists and more, all while better connecting them with friends, family or the online world. MSN Spaces, available in 30 markets and 15 languages, comes with a rich notification system that informs peoples contacts about changes to their Spaces to help bring people closer together."

Spaces is still in Beta and there are rumours of new features and interfaces as we write this in September, 2005.

The FaceBook

In an article in Business 2.0 in May 2005, Om Malik points out that "MySpace isn't the only startup to turn a Gen Y-based network into a moneymaking business. Mark Zuckerberg, a computer science major at Harvard, last year created a Web version of the freshman facebook, those student directories that serve as dating aids on campuses everywhere. Since it launched in February 2004, Zuckerberg's website, Thefacebook.com, has become a beehive for more than 2 million students at 430 colleges."

The site received at 4.3 million visitors in mid 2005, up from 2.5 million in January according to comScore Media Metrix. Now based in Palo Alto, California, it has so far received $13 million in funding from Excel.

Craigslist

Craigslist is seen as a phenomenon on the Internet. Built organically without any venture capital or funding, it continues to be a slightly unfashionable site with few graphics but densely packed with links to the content inside and there is much of it.

In June 2005 Randall Stross wrote in the New York Times – "These days, triple-digit annual growth rates are rare among major web sites. Meet that rarity: Craigslist. Exceptional, too, is the ability to draw 10 million unique visitors each month without ever relying on venture capital and equity markets. Or the ability to attain fourth place amongst general interest portals without ever spending a penny on marketing. Signal accomplishments, to be sure, fit for boasting in an annual report. But Craigslist is a privately held company that has no such reports, and no burning interest in the competitive fray. It does far more shrugging than boasting. Its management regard profits, which it has earned consistently since 1999, as merely the means to remain in control of its own destiny."

Is Craigslist a social networking site or a local newspaper classified ads section brought into the internet age? Newspapers see it as the latter and fear it as competition for their lifeblood revenue. Jim Buckmaster, in an interview with Fast Company magazine in late 2004, sees the Social Networking question thus: "I guess we're already there in a very light way. As far as adding technologies like friend of a friend, it is not something that we've looked at closely. In our view, it looks promising, but it's not a mature technology and we're probably going to be content to wait until it's been figured out. We figure it will filter up from the bottom of our site rather than a top-down approach. We'll look to weave it into Craigslist tapestry in an organic fashion over time rather than in some bold new initiative."

As noted earlier in this section, Craigslist recently acquired an unexpected shareholder when eBay bought a 25% stake. As Craig Newmark explains on his blog 'Craigsblog' when he incorporated Craigslist in 1999: "With the idea of establishing checks and balances, mostly on myself, I entrusted some equity in Craigslist to a guy who was working with me at the time. (I won't name him, out of respect for his privacy). I figured it didn't matter, since everyone agreed that the equity had only symbolic value, not dollar value. The guy later left the company, and decided to sell his equity, which I learned he had every legal right to do. He met with eBay and eBay in turn approached us to see how we would feel about them getting involved with us. Although I never figured that part of Craigslist might be owned by a public company, Meg Whitman and Pierre Omidyar showed that they were interested in us for all the right reasons."

There are many theories as to why eBay took that 25% stake. Randall Stross suggests that it is for knowledge transfer. "Executives at eBay have their own reasons to lie awake thinking about Craigslist. eBay, the child prodigy that went the corporate route and became a publicly traded company at the age of three, now faces sharply declining growth and that awful fate no prodigy is ever prepared for: middle age. Data collected by Nielsen/net ratings shows that eBay's page views in April 2005 grew by less than half a percentage point, compared with the previous April. At Craigslist, page views grew 130% in the same period. According to the company's data, its traffic is now about a fifth of eBay's. And the operational inefficiencies are outstanding: Craigslist has 18 employees, eBay has 8800."

Steve Rubel in his blog 'Micropersuasion' at the end of 2004 voices the other extreme of opinion: "In 2005 they will take this to the next level when eBay acquires the rest of Craigslist it doesn't yet own and then enables customers to blog right on their unified site. This will usher in a new era where citizen journalism is directly funded by person-to-person commerce." So far, over a year since the acquisition of the 25%, there are no signs of takeover.

Social Business and Business Networks

"Online networks are the new power lunch tables and the new golf courses for business life in the US. In the past 10 years, online dating has become mainstream; 40 million Americans use online dating sites. Now business people are starting to use the same family of technology to find business clients, new partners and jobs, through virtual contacts they make online." say David Teten and Scott Allen, observers of and participants in the networking scene, and co-authors of *The Virtual Handshake*, the 2005 book on the subject.

In the business networking space, alongside Ecademy which we describe as a social business network, there are three key networks: LinkedIn, Ryze and OpenBC, and we suggest that, in addition to Ecademy, you should join all three as they provide different dimensions and experiences in your networking. They are all very different. When combined with a VOIP solution like Skype, they provide a variety of networking options. Other networks such as Spoke, Tribe, Academici or Soflow can add further dimensions to your networking.

Simon Rogers, CEO of 2Delta in the UK, is a member of the big four networks, plus Soflow and many 'real-world' networks, too. He cautions against expecting to find customers directly from the networks. He finds 'door openers' there. "If I don't continually add to my network – the doors don't open. The activity never happens when you think it's going to happen, so you've got to keep on meeting people. If you concentrate on just three or four clients at a time, the tap turns off."

Jim Dickie, a journalist, gave a personal case study in 'destinationCRM' (an online magazine) in early 2005. Having already subscribed to, but never really used, LinkedIn, he chose to "delve into its application. Within LinkedIn I had 54 direct contacts that were part of my network. Since I was looking to interview existing vice presidents of sales, I typed that title into the search engine and found that my network could connect me with more than 500 current Vice Presidents of Sales within 3° of separation from me. On the surface this struck me as an impressive potential number, but would my contacts actually do an introduction for me?"

He chose 30 sales executives to interview, and used his LinkedIn contacts to facilitate an introduction to these people he had never met. "To my surprise 29 of these individuals accepted my request and passed it onto their contacts with a personal note of introduction." He was shocked when 23 of those targeted executives (including people in Europe and the Far East) accepted his request, and offered to consider helping with his research effort. "At this point I now had information on how to directly contact the sales execs. In following up with these individuals I was able to convince 18 of them to help me with my project. It equates to a 60% hit rate. Compared with results from cold calling, this is very impressive."

Diane Darling, president of Effective Networking Inc, a Boston consulting firm that teaches clients the value of networking, prefers face-to-face contact, reports Diane E. Lewis for the Boston Globe in May 2005. However, she has posted her name and shares business contacts on social networking sites like LinkedIn. Darling says that jobseekers should be aware that social networking can create a false sense of intimacy. For example, when she placed a note on the online bulletin board Craigslist.com indicating that she was looking for a bookkeeper, she received some unusual responses from people who didn't seem to understand that they were connecting to a potential employer.

Lewis also raises the issues of security. She quotes Chris Hoofnagle, director of the Electronic Privacy Information Centre (EPIC), who counsels caution. "Lots of people are engaging in this networking behaviour and do not know that there are companies that scrape the site for information. They save the information to sell to strangers." His group is lobbying for stricter laws. "If the goal is to engage in networking, then there should be rules that say the information could only be used for certain purposes and that it must be destroyed after a certain amount of time, such as when you actually get that job," he said.

Regardless of the security issues, being found on business networks has become crucial for some connections. Scott Allen on the Virtual Handshake blog 'LinkedIn or Locked Out' quotes the case of Paul Allen, Managing Partner of US business incubator InfoBase ventures, who likes to help entrepreneurs with advice on business plans and raising capital. "But as a frequent lecturer at business schools and conferences, he recently found himself inundated with requests. So he made a new rule: if you're not a member of the LinkedIn network with a minimum of 10 connections and two endorsements on the site, don't even bother calling him. "The most important thing for an entrepreneur is not necessarily what they know, but who they know," says Allen."

"If you're not linked in, you're locked out" continues Scott Allen. "These tools are no longer a curiosity – they are quickly becoming 'how business is done'. Entrepreneurs are using them to connect with investors, strategic partners, board members, prospective customers and potential employees – the entire spectrum." The article suggests two key advantages of the tools:

- accelerating the speed at which companies can get to the decision maker

- levelling the field by replacing costly middlemen small business can ill afford.

As we write this book, O'Reilly, the San Francisco-based publisher of technical IT books and provider of training and conferences, launched the 'O'Reilly Connection' in beta. This network caters for the software development community. In the press release accompanying the launch, Tim O'Reilly, CEO and founder said, "I've been fascinated by the possibilities of social networking, but frustrated by the need to build up social network databases from scratch rather than by instrumenting the real social networks that occur in the course of our daily life. We have an active community at O'Reilly, people who read and write our books, who attend and speak at our conferences, and who read and write for the O'Reilly Network. And one of the 'back channel' conversations among all these people is about finding developers to hire, or to help with projects. Could a social networking application help us facilitate these conversations? The O'Reilly Connection is our first stab at answering this question."

LinkedIn

LinkedIn (www.linkedin.com) is a huge repository of profiles, well over 4.5 million and growing. Started by Reid Hoffman and Konstantin Guericke, LinkedIn really took off when it received

$4.7 million of venture capital in 2003 allowing it to build rapidly. Business Week in March 2005 puts total venture capital received by Linkedin at $14 million. Linkedin noted that they raised $10million in a round of venture funding in late 2004 and also acknowledged that it has received angel funding as well. There is now a little social interaction on the site through 'affinity clubs' but it is mostly an excellent way of locating and contacting (via people you already know) targeted people in corporations or smaller businesses worldwide. It is also possible to use random approaches to people in similar industries or who are friends of friends.

From an initial model where everything was free, Linkedin have added some premium services whilst keeping the basic service – listing a profile, connecting with people within three degrees – free. InMails cost $10 each and allows users to connect with Linkedin users who are three degrees or more from them or who do not appear in their network. Job advertising is also carried on the site, with each ad costing $95 – though there are introductory prices. Revenue is believed to be running at around $200,000 per annum with a roughly 50/50 split between subscriptions and advertising.

Senior Executives, and those who attract many approaches, like the network because it allows them to manage those approaches. Connections are effected through those who are already connected to the target person and the system calculates the possible ways in which a request may be relayed through intermediaries. Along with the request to contact will be a short note explaining why the connection is needed. The target (or any intermediary) can refuse to accept or forward the request.

In a 2004 interview with nPost, Hoffman explained his thinking when, at PayPal, he first had the idea for LinkedIn: "We were also trying to hire a flash designer at PayPal. I realised that the key issue that brings the 'haves' and the 'have-nots' together is personal recommendations. When someone approaches a 'have' they are recommended. The problem with being a 'have' is that tons and tons of people want you to invest with them. They get over-whelmed by the noise and the question is how to sort through the noise to find the signals. It is a similar picture for jobs. Companies such as eBay, Google, Apple, etc. are all inundated with job appli-cants. They are trying to identify which resumes they should pay more attention to. The tried and trusted answer is to look at those resumes that come recommended by people that the hiring indi-vidual knows and trusts."

In the same interview Hoffman explains his view that the growth of LinkedIn is exactly because they don't allow any social interac-tions. "The sites tend to go to the lowest common denominator, so if you tend to use the site for personal as well as professional usage, you end up getting a quasi-personal site." The growth of LinkedIn, he says, is because "we are focused on the profes-sional, it is targeted for business people. Our message is clear and concise, which is why we have seen our phenomenal growth. This helps people better understand what they are inviting their friends and contacts to join. They know what they are being invited to. With our site there is a clear understanding of who you should invite. Whereas other sites that combine business and personal networking don't appeal to professionals who are also married, as the value is not as clear to them."

MyLinkedinPowerForum (MLPF), which is a Yahoo Group run by Vincent Wright, provides an outlet for discussion about Linkedin and is visited by members of the Management Team.

Ryze

Ryze (www.ryze.com/) was launched in October, 2001 by Adrian Scott who used it to supplement the face to face 'mixers' he ran in San Francisco for Finance sector people. It has since outgrown those roots and has, according to its own information, more than 250,000 members in more than 200 countries. Ryze's ambition is to be "a place where professionals from all industries can come together, network, expand their spheres of influence and do business."

The Ryze formula is a mixture of face-to-face and online contact building. There are events throughout the world which are particularly strong in the US where the network began. The online site allows access to event information, allows members to connect with each other and exchange private messages. It also offers clubs, which members can start or join, to allow threaded conversations on a topic and classified advertising.

openBC

From its early origins in Germany, openBC (http://www.openbc.com/) has grown rapidly in a short time to have over 1 million members, approximately 60,000 of them subscribers, communicating in 16 languages across the world. Members can create profiles, start and join clubs. As many as 12,000 members may be online at any time. There is, however, no central place where you can address that online community directly. openBC has ambitious targets and aims to reach 10 million members by 2007. New features will be delivered on the site and on the 'white label' sites that openBC also powers (for example Academici – networking for the academic community) and on http://mobile.openbc.com.

openBC was founded by Lars Heinrich, now CEO and Bill Liao, now the COO. Bill explains "openBC was designed with one context in mind: to be a platform focussed on the need of business people to more efficiently come together to grow their sphere of influence in their business community." Those principles determine how the software is developed and the experience of the user. "The default settings of our network for an invited guest (being invited ensures you get the free trial period of premium membership) are all set to make a new member open and in the very first login everyone is asked to select the privacy setting that suits them. The vast majority of people choose to continue to be open and we have found that it is the fact that they can opt, at any time, to put up safety barriers, that allows them the freedom to be open. After the context of business the security is actually the biggest factor in allowing people to feel free to approach one another."

In the spirit, as he puts it "of a clear context and freedom", Bill also explains that openBC allows people to define and manage their own events and forums and provides an extensive toolset for both of these functions that they are continually upgrading. "These functions are not simple and they are worth exploring and all of this functionality is 100% free of charge." he adds.

Ecademy

Ecademy (www.ecademy.com) also offers its members the opportunity the opportunity to create their personal profile, to build a network, to blog, to add listings and to join clubs to discuss matters of common interest. Through the home page of the network, members can also blog about topics of interest or highlight their offer or requirements using the MarketStar feature. After eight years (1998 – 2006) of development, Ecademy is poised for the next phase of its journey. A new look to the site was delivered in late 2005 and this book you currently hold in your hands is also part of that journey. We tell the story of Ecademy and its key characters in more detail in the next chapter.

Government Networking Initiatives

Government agencies are beginning to recognise the need to network, and are setting up schemes for smaller business. In the UK, Business Link (part of the Small Business Service) in Hampshire began Business Xchange, a networking service that meets monthly. In the US, David Teten notes in the Virtual Handshake blog in July 2005, that the Small Business Administration has begun a business matchmaking service online. "Business matchmaking is a partnership between the US Small Business Administration and HP, matching small companies with federal, state, and local government agencies and large corporations that have actual contract opportunities for products and services offered by smaller companies. The program's goal is to stimulate jobs and growth of small business by taking advantage of opportunities that are normally relegated to distinct geographical areas such as the Washington, DC beltway or a city where a major corporation is located."

Teten notes that business matchmaking combines education and counselling by experts, business advisers and topical experts with networking and matchmaking through regional face-to-face events. In addition to the regional face-to-face events, the business matchmaking online network is being introduced in five pilot communities. This will provide telephone-based interviews after electronic matching between small businesses and procurement representatives.

The SBA note that since the programme began, three years ago, business matchmaking has matched small-business sellers with procurement representative buyers in more than 23,000 appointments, resulting in more than $26 million in contracts. In addition, business matchmaking has received significant support by the media that helps the SBA communicate the availability of this free program for small business.

5 *Ecademy*

Ecademy (www.Ecademy.com) differs from most of the networks discussed in two crucial ways. Firstly, it has its origins in the UK while most of the others (openBC excepted) are US (often Silicon Valley) based. Secondly, it has developed over the eight years to 2006 as an organic business. It has had no VC money at all, in a type of business that tends to consume dollars at an alarming rate. As Thomas Power, chairman of Ecademy, puts it: "What we've done with Ecademy is impossible on the amount of capital we've had. Fear of failure and sheer persistence has made it happen."

As we write this in late 2005, Ecademy is approaching 70,000 members, of whom more than 10% subscribe to one of the membership schemes. The focus is on Social Business Networking because the members of the management team see relationship building as an important part of the process of doing business. Members are encouraged to interact socially, a process that often leads to business opportunities.

Ecademy is a Social Business Network built around a web-based platform (www.Ecademy.com) that allows members to communicate with each other through blogs (personal weblogs), marketplace listings, articles, private messages and clubs.

Development and Growth

In 1998, Thomas Power was just starting out on a self-employed journey as a speaker, consultant and writer. Penny Power, Thomas's wife and a successful businesswoman in her own right, noticed that ongoing support was a major need for Thomas and for others taking that journey. Anyone leaving a corporate job would be likely to miss the support and companionship that such an organization provides. As a newly self-employed consultant, Thomas was having to do the whole job himself without Finance, IT, HR and all the other supports of corporate life. Being self-employed is often a very lonely life. There was nowhere to go simply to chat to other people, to bounce off ideas or exchange news and information.

On 7th February, 1998, over pizza in the Surrey town of Farnham, Penny set out her initial idea for a place where the self-employed could support each other and find ways of working together. Ecademy began as a meeting of people from Thomas's network at a bar in Central London. There were no speeches, no celebrities, just "Chardonnay and conversation". The attendees seemed to like the format and suggested meeting again in a month. On that occasion, Penny invited attendees to bring a friend – a formula repeated successfully ever since. Many took that message to heart, brought friends and colleagues and numbers quickly increased. The idea began to evolve. As Penny remembers, "It wasn't a financially planned business. It was an endeavour to combine business acumen with helping people."

Penny turned to Glenn Watkins (now Chief Executive) with whom she had worked, successfully, at Hand Technologies to help her develop the idea. The initial Ecademy website was developed with the objective of "connecting business people to network and develop careers around the Internet marketplace". Glenn remembers this time as being, if anything, too easy. "It started out as a euphoric journey with the excitement of setting up a new business, working with Penny. Maybe we were naive, and building as we went along, but that was how it was for Internet businesses then."

As Penny remembers it, "From the inception of Ecademy, we wanted to build a business network for members to learn, network and develop their businesses in a place that they could enjoy, make friends and have the comfort of knowing the management care about each member and their careers and business". Penny's vision was to "start a business network for people like us to connect with one another, spreading emotional and financial wealth around the globe".

From the very start, Ecademy was more than a web site. "We held an off-line meeting within three months of the site going live in March 1999; 27 members came along and they loved it. The next month, 60 members came along, and so on" remembers Penny. Between launch and the dot-com bust, Stephen Clarke, a personal investor in Ecademy was MD with Thomas Power as Chairman.

Like many Internet businesses at the time, Ecademy began working towards IPO (Initial Public Offering) and a date of 18th March 2000 was set. Investors were found to fund the IPO activity and funds of over £800,000 were raised. A further £500,000 was put into the business by management during 1998 and 1999. On the 13th March, the market began to fall rapidly and the IPO was cancelled. The capital raised had been spent and Ecademy faced a future that was, to say the least, uncertain. Meetings slowed down from a peak of over 250 people to around 30 to 40, and a period of retrenchment began.

Ecademy briefly became an e-learning portal but during 2001 became a networking site. Glenn comments, "Networking had always been intrinsic to the business but we made the decision to make it central, to put it slap bang in the middle. Our strapline changed to "connecting business people", the strapline still used today. Our plan was to connect people to other people, to knowledge, to support and to business transactions. They would be interdependent." This change, driven by the intense pain of the dot-com crash, marked the start of Ecademy as we know it today.

Julian Bond, now CTO, began to rewrite the website in 2001, basing his work on the open source tool Drupal. The site that came from this revision has recently been updated but has been the bedrock for the development of Ecademy over the past three years. Many of the functions in use on the Ecademy site come from this period of development and provide signature features of the site.

During this process, a number of key lessons were learnt. Penny discovered that Ecademy is an organic business that adapts naturally. "We realised that this was no ordinary business on the net, this was a community that wanted to network, wanted to have a place to go for this, and through their content and messaging they could swing this community away from attracting e-business people into attracting business people and they could create the community they wanted and needed."

In early 2002, Ecademy introduced blogging on the site and members were, for the first time, able to share their thoughts and opinions with all other members. Blogging has been one of the key developments that has shaped Ecademy's development. Blogs still appear on the Front Page of Ecademy.

During 2002, Ecademy management were watching the network grow rapidly without it earning sufficient money to pay for itself. There had to be a way to make the website pay its way. Towards the end of 2002, the team came up with the idea of PowerNetworkers. PowerNetworkers would subscribe to the service in return for additional services that were not available to the non-subscribing members. On December 7th, 2002, PowerNetworking began and over a period of months, subscribers began to increase.

At the time, movement from free to fee on the Internet was still quite new and somewhat controversial. However, the number of PowerNetworkers has increased steadily since introduction.

In March 2003, Ecademy took over Beyond Bricks, a DTI project, and Mike Southon came on board to manage the community. Beyond Bricks became the first 'Trusted Network' with its own content and front page. Mike Southon, author of 'The Beermat Entrepreneur', still runs the network, now renamed as 'Beermat Ecademy'.

In October 2003, Paul Sherman, a longstanding Ecademy member, created the first marketplace for Ecademy. It was initially built 'off platform' on Paul's 'Broaden' site. It was soon moved on to the Ecademy platform to make it easier for members to use. The initial marketplace built up to 350 revenue-sharing vendors of products and services and many free listings.

Clubs were launched by Glenn Watkins and Julian Bond in December 2003. Clubs can be created by any PowerNetworker™ in order to discuss specific topics of interest. "We went to bed, and in the morning there were 27 clubs formed in different parts of the world with different interests and there were a couple of clubs based on their towns", Penny recalls. Clubs now represent a major part of the activity on Ecademy. There are almost 2,000 clubs on the platform, some more active than others. Ecademy Regional clubs allow Ecademists in a specific area to get together on and, importantly, off line. There are Ecademy clubs in many parts of the world and more will be opening in the next few years.

At the end of 2004 and into 2005, a number of key changes took place.

In September, 2004, Ecademy introduced a formalised complaints system, allowing members to express their dissatisfaction with the behaviour or language used by another member. The complaints system is triggered by the use of the 'complain' link in the offending member's profile.

Ecademy decided to place some offending members in Ecademy Jail. The Ecademy Jail was a (normally) temporary punishment applied to those who did not abide by the Ecademy Terms and Conditions and consisted of a suspension of access rights for a period of time. It was primarily intended to provide a cooling-off period while the person concerned considered what they were doing. Ecademy Jail was disbanded in late 2005 as part of a review of the Ethos and Best Practice on Ecademy, and the complaints system became fully automated under the control of Penny Power.

Complaints can be made for a number of reasons :
- abusive behaviour
- spam
- blatant selling in blogs
- MLM/Network Marketing (which is banned in Ecademy)
- Faked or false identity
- 419 (advance fee fraud) scams.

Penny is supported in her monitoring of the community by Mentors, who have stepped forward from the community, to provide support to management to ensure the smooth running of the community. All mentors are named on the site and are happy to work with members to help them avoid infringing the Ethos and Best Practice Guide.

BlackStar Life Membership was launched in November 2004. Life Membership was an early form of a chargeable club. It sought to provide a subset of Ecademists with access to a mutually-supportive environment with special attention from Thomas Power and Roger Hamilton. Benefits are beginning to flow after a year of operation. Members are part of a pre-selected and filtered community where there is considerable energy. In the positive environment, BlackStars find it easy to network with, and trust, other members. There are now over 200 BlackStars based around the world, who meet regularly and communicate using the Ecademy platform. There is an objective of growing the BlackStar numbers steadily over the coming years.

GreenStar membership was introduced in December 2004 as an alternative to PowerNetworking. The access given to GreenStar Members is less than for PowerNetworkers but more than 'Guest Members' who still pay nothing to access the service.

In early 2005, Marketplace came to the homepage. At the same time, a new membership level, MarketStar, was created. The new Front Page was set out with community on the left and commerce on the right or, as Thomas puts it, "blogging on the left and flogging on the right". It was launched on 6th May, 2005 at £50 per month for MarketStar membership. There was a 30 day free trial and MarketStar was included as an additional benefit to BlackStars. On 1st July the price moved to £25 per month and there was an immediate uplift in the numbers to 40 paid subscribers by mid-July.

On December 1st, 2005, all of the MarketStar benefits were added to the PowerNetworker membership, making the PN package much more valuable whilst holding the price. MarketStar listings now go to GoogleBase, often within 60 minutes, giving those members who list products and services a reach well beyond Ecademy itself.

Ecademy has grown under the direction of Thomas Power (Chairman), Glenn Watkins (Chief Executive) and Penny Power (Founder and Director). Julian Bond as CTO has been responsible for developing the Ecademy.com web platform which underpins online networking at Ecademy. Andrew Widgery (Global & UK Development Manager) has been influential in the development of the geographical structure of Ecademy. Paul Sherman has developed the Marketplace listings service and Léon Benjamin has provided many insights and ideas including that of 'Winning by Sharing'.

Ecademy has been developed organically over eight years with investment coming from shareholders who continue to have a close interest in the business. Members of management have invested significantly, for some time forgoing salary from the business.

Ecademy has been learning on the move – what Thomas calls 'live R&D'. It hasn't been a planned journey, indeed, "had we mapped the journey out, had we created a business plan, had we brought in large investors, Ecademy would not be here today", comments

Penny. "Ecademy would not have made any business sense at all, the time and money that has gone into it would have terrified us."

Ecademy membership, measured by the number of profiles maintained on the website has grown steadily from 1998 when there were 750 members, through 2000 with 3000 members, 2002 with 12,000 members and 48,000 members in 2004. There were around 67,000 members at the end of 2005.

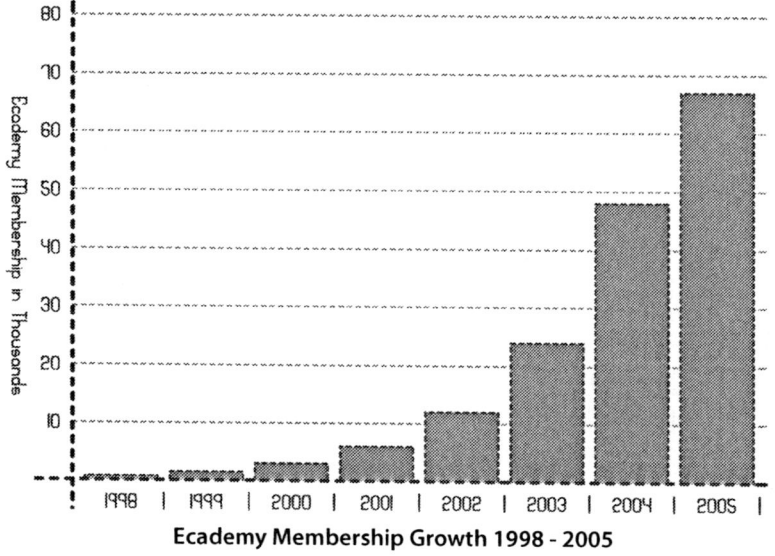

Ecademy Membership Growth 1998 - 2005

In the period January to June 2005, 12,000 new members joined Ecademy of whom 3,000 joined at one of the subscription levels – a level of 25% subscribing. 70% of subscribers use the system every month indicating a growing loyalty to the site. Around 50 blogs and 30 MarketStar entries are added each day. Many members spend substantial amounts of time on the site suggesting a certain level of dependency. There is currently strong growth in a number of international sectors including Northern Europe.

In the third quarter of 2005 the number of subscribers reached 8,000. The aim to reach 10,000 subscribers by the end of 2005 was missed but ambition is still high and "in 2006 we would ideally like to reach 20,000 subscribers," notes Thomas Power, "although we recognise that this is a huge task".

It has been an experience that has had its highs and lows. The founders and management have learnt that they must be responsible for and available to the members. "Some Internet businesses seem to think they can behave differently to off-line business", comments Penny. "Can you imagine your customers not being able to reach you if they were unhappy with your service or product? If they were abused by another one of your customers? Of course not. You're responsible for your product."

Culture

Ecademy is a Social Business Network. The order of the words in that phrase is crucial. It is Social before Business, Friendship before Trade, Community ahead of Commerce. It is based on the important understanding that 'people refer, recommend or buy from people they like'. The more valuable the trade, the more trust will be needed to make it happen. The more open you are and the more experiences and interests you share, the more trust will develop.

Ecademy is a culture, a series of customs and codes that the majority follow. It consists of a series of practices that everyone respects, participates in and helps to advance. It is a belief system, of course, but NOT a religion or a cult. Ecademy is a microcosm of society online. In developmental terms, Ecademy is probably at a green 'communitarian/egalitarian' stage in Spiral Dynamics (see Chapter 12 for more). Moving networks in general up the developmental spiral to the second tier, yellow, integrative level, is addressed at the end of the book. There are some potentially huge benefits in doing so.

Ecademy has been built around the principle of 'winning by sharing'. This means that it is not a place where 'every man for himself' will work. What you get out of Ecademy is related to what you put in. It is a community where 'gives' are more valued than 'takes'. The more you give, the more you are likely to receive but the giving needs to be unconditional for this to work.

When members were able to blog, it quickly became apparent that many of the blogs and stories on the site were not business related. Penny notes "We were stunned by the generous acts that people made to one another, to help others grow their businesses and this is when a light went on in my head. People want emotional wealth just as much, if not more than financial wealth. In a fragmented sometimes cruel world, it is great to know that there are others that care." Emotional Wealth has become a major part of the Ecademy offering, filling a need that is there in many members to deal with loneliness and pain.

Nevertheless, Ecademy is still a business network and makes the assumption that everyone is honest and professional. Ecademy is not a chat room or social club; it is a serious business network. However, to build a strong business relationship, members must first gain trust from one another through having a personal relationship. This is critical before you can expect to move on to a relationship where a transaction can take place. Remember that networking is not selling or personal promotion.

Despite the growing number of options for connecting made available by technology, people can be professionally lonely. Whether it is that technology causes isolation or the media create paranoia, community is being broken down. Thomas Power sees Ecademy's role as reinforcing community because "community makes you feel safe, and when you feel safe you want to do stuff. Not necessarily trade, but trade will be one of the possibilities. If you feel safe, you encourage people to come and join you". Ecademy is just one global village among thousands online. "It is our village and we have made it our own and continue to have to make it our own, as there is nothing else for us or anyone helping us. We are on our own, and must make the best job we can".

Development of Ecademy has taken what Penny calls "the long ethical route", not taking investment from those who would muddy the waters, forcing the network to take on volumes of members that would have the wrong intentions. "We have kept close to the members, Glenn, Thomas, Julian and I have always been only an e-mail or a meeting away. We are honest and transparent, we have high morals and a belief in the way people should communicate in the business world. We want you to make friends, feel safe and enjoy the humour here. Therefore we must keep it moral and clean. It has to be a place where members do not risk being abused or ridiculed," notes Penny.

There are many views of what Ecademy is. For some it is a place to manage and make contacts; for others it is an online magazine to which they can, if they choose, contribute; others join for the clubs and the ability to discuss matters of joint interest at length and leisure; others see it as a marketplace where vendors offer wide ranges of goods and services to a growing community, while groups of members find it a place to build and develop alliances to pitch for and win business. For them, Ecademy is the virtual office in which they can meet and work together, even though they are geographically distributed, the virtual enterprise. For most of us it is a combination of those things and more.

Ecademy can be considered a management system for three important 'Cs' of online networking – contacts, conversations, and community. Rather than trying to sell to contacts in the initial exchanges, the key is in developing trust and deeper conversation. From these conversations, community will build. The opportunities provided by geographical clubs for members to meet each other face to face will help this process develop more quickly.

Social Capital and Citizen Journalism

When we interact online in a Social or Business network, when we create or comment upon a blog, when we add our photos to a site like Flickr, when we bookmark and tag web pages and resources in a public site like del.ico.us, we are creating Social Capital. Social Capital, says David Halpern in his 2005 book of that name, sits alongside financial capital, physical capital, tangible assets and human capital. He describes it as "social networks and the norms and sanctions that govern their character. It is valued for its potential to facilitate individual and community action, especially through the solution of collective action problems."

The tools that are being delivered across the Internet allow us to share our lives, interests and business with anyone who finds them interesting. Our words and pictures are published to a large audience using simple tools. Getting those words and pictures noticed is harder but, nonetheless, possible.

According to Dan Gillmor, author of the book *We, The Media*, we are becoming citizen journalists – though most of us are columnists and only very few get read widely. Nevertheless, pictures from mobile phones are reaching the world's media and giving true eyewitness experience of hard news items – the 7th July bombs in London and the 1st October bombs in Bali are both examples of amateur footage spreading around the world's media. The

BBC in London actively sought out such material and all of it was turned over to police investigators who, with the addition of CCTV material, literally patched together a composite picture of what happened.

The adoption of standards like RSS (really simple syndication) allows aggregation of the available news and feature feeds from professional and amateur sources to create searchable resources such as Technorati and Google Blogsearch. Thus from the millions of words created every day in blogs, some sense and order can be created. As searching and matching technologies improve, the idea of a daily newspaper *The Daily Me* filled only with items of interest to you comes closer. However, Thomas cautions that too much personalisation will lead to a narrow view of news and opinions that may result in missed opportunities.

In the Googlezon video, Robin Sloan and Matt Thompson envisage a nightmare world where "everyone contributes in some way. Everyone participates to create a living, breathing mediascape. However, the Press, as you know it, has ceased to exist. The Fourth Estate's fortunes have waned. 20th Century news organizations are an after-thought, a lonely remnant of a not-too-distant past." Contributors (newsmasters in Sloane and Thompson's terminology) get paid by the popularity of their contributions, and the level of reporting has descended to the lowest common denominator. In this negative scenario, Googlezon (the eventual merger of Google and Amazon after they have consolidated most other providers) has become the sole source of information (and misinformation) for most of the planet. Printed newspapers, such as the New York Times, have ceased publication.

However far-fetched you might consider Googlezon, the old media outlets are taking this threat seriously. According to the Financial Times in May 2005, "the World Association of Newspapers, the trade body representing 1300 publishers, will today call for a more coherent strategy to defend the industry from the threat of free online news, search engines and price erosion. The association's annual congress, opening in Seoul, will be told the reports of an industry-wide malaise have been exaggerated and that more titles will need to embrace new technology." The article goes on to note that global newspaper sales rose by 2% in 2004 to almost 400 million copies a day, in spite of intense competition and volatile advertising demand in many countries. Overall advertising revenues also rose by more than 5%. But the industry's share of global advertising has remained flat at 30%. Most of the growth in 2004 however came from emerging markets in Asia, South America and Africa, while newspaper sales fell in North America and Europe.

Social networks and sites like eBay, Craigslist and GoogleBase are also threatening the economic basis on which local newspapers exist. A June 2005 article 'What eBay could learn from Craigslist' by Randall Stross in the New York Times, notes that "local newspapers have derived 30 to 50% of their advertising revenue from the classifieds. Surprisingly, the momentum of this online alternative with virtually free offerings had not drawn much attention as recently as last fall, when Creative Intelligence surveyed the newspaper industry. They discovered that many executives were unaware of the arrival of Craigslist in their own cities. Nor were all aware that aside from a sliver, ads on Craigslist were available free." The article notes that one major player in the U. S. local newspaper market, Knight Ridder, "announced its plan to finesse the challenge of free classifieds: it dropped fees for ads for merchandise posted on the websites of 22 of its newspapers. When you visit one of these sites prepared to submit an ad, however, you must navigate past pitches for various fee-based upgrades. The basic is free, but after 500 characters, you pay $1.99. Boldface is another $1.99. A photo package $3.99. And so on. A la carte charges are the way business is done on eBay but not on the Commons of Craigslist. What part of 'free' is difficult to understand?"

It's not just local newspapers. News Corporation, one of the largest media groups in the world, called its managers together in late 2005 to work on their strategy for new media – the second time they had discussed this in the six months. The acquisition of Intermix Media, including mySpace, for $629 million by News Corporation to form a major element in Fox interactive media shows that money will be no object in the creation of a new media offering to rival or harness the power of the fast-growing citizen media. In early 2006, they appointed 33-year-old Jeremy Philips to the Office of the Chairman with a brief to look at strategy across the company with emphasis on overseeing Internet investments. Philips will report directly to Rupert Murdoch.

The big media owners – record companies, movie studios, hybrid media owners like News Corporation, Time Warner and Sony – have been concerned by the speed with which technology that allows faithful copies of their product to be made has become available to all. Their activities have included pursuing the copiers, including teenagers and younger children, to insist on copyright payment and seeking to achieve favourable legislation. An attempt to get the concept of a 'Broadcast Flag' into US law failed in 2005. Further attempts to have digital rights protected by law are happening in Europe and, again, in the US. Opposition has come from bodies like the Electronic Frontier Foundation and individuals like Cory Doctorow. The laws seek to compel manufacturers of digital equipment to recognise and act upon code in the media which would prevent copying or enforce other digital rights such as number of uses.

An implementation of Digital Rights Management by Sony Music in 2005, by implementing software (called a rootkit) on Windows PCs that allowed files to be hidden, caused widespread condemnation as hackers created an exploit to use the hiding mechanism to place unwanted files on to computers. In true citizen journalism tradition, the news of this was broken on a blog by Mark Russinovich, who provided a very detailed background to the problem and its solution.

Blogging has taken off worldwide with 40,000 new blogs being added every day and 9 million blogs available to read, according to Business Week in May 2005. By August, just three months later, Technorati report that they were tracking 14.2 million blogs and over 1.3 billion links. This, they report, represents a doubling of blogs from March 2005 – just five months. They note that "the blogosphere continues to double about every 5.5 months". Growth is now 2 million blogs a month.

In the January 2004, Stowe Boyd writing in Darwin Magazine said "I predict that 2004 will be a year when will see the successful linkage between rich content systems – like salesforce automation applications, corporate knowledge management applications and blogs, as only the most obvious examples – with social network tools. This will certainly not be 'social tools Nirvana'. It will be years before interoperability and effective standards are in wide use, but we will see the initial hurdles of context and content surmounted. At least in part." What he saw may be happening more slowly than he suggests, but be certain that it is happening.

As more people enter the world of freelancing, there will need to be reliable ways of obtaining sufficient work to meet income and development goals. Networks have a major role here.

Social business networks will become the matching engines of the freeformers generation. They will provide project owners with the ability to define opportunities and freelance workers with the ability to specify their needs and skill sets. Then the network can match their requirements and send offers to the freelancers that they may choose to take up. It is a difficult process to manage. Matching available work with available skills is a model much used by professional consulting and services firms who have some advantages over freelance networks.

Nonetheless, the day will come, Thomas Power believes, when you can log on to LinkedIn or openBC or Ecademy and there, in your inbox, will be the offers of work that you need for the next three to six months. "I see that my job is not to have a pretty website and offline events with Chardonnay but to put work on every member's table internationally" he says. "Global Labour Matching in real-time is the future of work and the future of networks including Ecademy."

How we achieve this will be less easy to do than to say. There have been many attempts to make independent freelance networks effective. Most have been based on the models of larger consultancy groups. Projects are defined and sold by a team of people who then hand the project to a small team to identify and allocate the right resources. This model works when used by larger firms for a number of reasons:

- they can afford to put the sales teams out there and pay them

- their teams are made up from a pool of consultants who are employed and paid whatever their work status

- they use quiet times for consultants to invest in training courses and 'on-the-job training' by adding them (as additional free resources or in a lower-level role) to teams in the field

- they can and do charge a premium that allows them to carry enough redundancy within teams to ensure that they can respond quickly to new requirements.

When applied to freelance groups, however, there are problems that must be overcome, and often they are not.

- very few team members are motivated to sell on behalf of the team

- the allocation team does not exist or is staffed by volunteers

- it is not a simple process to match consultants in the pool to requirements and to check availability, especially as those consultants are also marketing themselves in other ways

- quiet times for specific consultants will be periods of no income and, usually, no training either; they become disillusioned and move on

- independent networks charge less for their time because they are perceived by the market – or perceive themselves – to be less valuable than the bigger firms, as a result they have no way of paying their members in slack periods.

- buyers often select larger firms for their reputation and size.

To achieve our goal, therefore, some or all of these issues will need to be addressed. The network needs to attract enough providers of project work to make it worthwhile for potential team members to sign up. Some providers will also be project team members at different times. The ability to create the project requirement outline to ensure that there are the right skills available may help the tendering process. When a project is won, a further process to identify, cost and contract the teams will be crucial. The system will have to be capable of finding substitutes, should the original team members be unavailable. Much depends on the detailed information being held and the accuracy with which it is completed. The matching system will also be crucial.

There are many schemes that are, in one way or another, addressing this issue. Ki work, founded by Michael Wolff, has been created to help ki workers, the same people we have referred to as free-formers, to find work as part of virtual project teams. According to its website, "ki work is a new and competitive form of outsourcing work to a flexible, distributed and self-organising workforce:

- It provides a collaborative network for outsourcing work to individuals and teams who are motivated and independent

- It is enabled by technologies which distribute business appl-ications and information across companies, individual agents and customers e.g. broadband and on-line collaborative plat-forms

- It is suitable for white-collar processes currently performed in call centres and back office departments, employing 20-30% of the UK workforce."

Ki work is needed because "both the nature of employment and service to customers are changing. Employers and workers are increasingly faced with the need to reduce transaction costs, access a highly skilled and stable workforce that is currently under-employed or remote from work centres, to stop the flow of work to offshore destinations like India and increase the personalisation of services to customers". A global version of ki work, of course, might be proposing work flowing to India and other developing parts of the world.

The structure of ki work is important and reminiscent of the 'big firm' structure we discuss above. Process owners (the entrepreneurs in the scheme) who wish to employ or contract with white collar workers in a variety of industries talk to outsource service providers, have access to a pool of available ki workers and can offer them work with the process owners. Two other stakeholders complete the picture. Social funders provide grant assistance and other support, while service providers make the whole activity possible through broadband services, technical platforms and training.

Mike Burnage, supported by the Academy of Chief Executives, has formed the WisdomBank to stem the "loss of knowledge and experience" caused by five hundred thousand people who leave the work place annually through retirement. "This resultant loss of is an unacceptable waste of a valuable resource, and as a nation we are all the poorer for it".

WisdomBank facilitates access to this pool of knowledge by matching WisdomSeekers to WisdomGivers. WisdomGivers are mature, experienced, professional individuals, possibly retired or now in a portfolio career, who have years of knowledge and experience to share, while WisdomSeekers could be entrepreneurs starting or developing new businesses, managers of organisations or institutions, or indeed anyone who could benefit from access to additional knowledge and advice.

"WisdomBank enables access to experienced advisors, who offer a multitude of skills as and when needed, at a fraction of the cost of conventional agencies or consultants."

Ecademy Corporate Services (ECS) has been set up, as a joint venture with Ecademy, to work with organisations who need to use networking inside their business. ECS will help companies to meet the challenges caused by fewer face-to-face conversations, as a result of more staff working from home or being distributed over a wider geographical distance. Here, networking can be used to generate a more open culture of communication inside the business. This leads to online communities that help staff share expertise and best practice, provide peer groups; and help deal with problems or unusual circumstances.

The need for networking also arises as organisations outsource and tender for more of their activities. Communication from inside the corporation of tomorrow will meet with the external world, and this will require it to interact with greater numbers of people than is the case today. Together, the organisation and its outsourcing partners need to establish high levels of trust, a community identity, and have the ability to sense and respond to both expected and unexpected situations.

Where tenders are developed, the organisation will need to be more effective at matching their prospects' needs to its own and its partners' capabilities. Here, networking can be used to improve the process of building the right team and the right solution for a successful bid.

LinkedIn have launched a job listings service but, at present, it is more of a classified advertising service than matching. The first successful Global Labour Matching service to market (they're not there yet...) will be able to capitalise on first mover advantage. However, as Google proved, they will still be vulnerable to a later, better service.

Networks and Innovation

Can networks provide a place where innovation can flourish? Are the thousands of messages and other daily interchanges, simply adding hot air, or do they result in new ideas, new possibilities, new businesses?

Our own observations over eight years of Ecademy is that many new businesses have been created – some successful and some less so – by the meeting of minds through the network. Collaborative tools have been improving alongside the networks. Tools like Skype and Avecomm, allow members to communicate across great distances at very low cost.

The publisher of this book, Ecademy Press, was formed following networking meetings, including one following a 'netwalk'. Networking really does trigger innovation and encourage new businesses.

Hungry Week is another good example of a network-delivered innovation. The initial idea came from a number of sources, including a blog on Ecademy about the imbalance between hunger in the third world and over-consumption in the first. A project team was formed using Ecademy as a rallying point. Members of the team were distributed across the world and came together through club messages on Ecademy and instant chats using Skype. By using Skype chats, the meetings were self-documenting. From its beginnings in February, 2005, Hungry Week built an external website and recruited members to live on less than 1,000 calories per day during the week 13th – 19th June, 2005.

The Flame Institute is another example of how networking, serendipity and a positive attitude can make things happen. It all started when Tom Evans put the wrong type of fuel in his car on the way to a netwalk. Tom was planning to return 60 miles home with his vehicle but Thomas Power kindly offered Tom a lift home at the end of the netwalk. Tom was left for an hour and half waiting for the recovery vehicle and finally reconnected with the netwalk at lunchtime at a pub, after a solo 5-mile trek. There was only one seat left – next to Nick Heap. So three events had conspired to connect Tom and Nick – Tom's error with the fuel, Thomas Power's memory for not only people but their cars and Nick's appreciation of Tom's positive attitude in not turning round and going back. You can imagine that by this time Tom could not keep his error secret and much ribbing ensued. This was serendipity indeed.

Tom and Nick got talking and Nick introduced Tom to the concept of Core Process, a method of helping people find their true purpose. Nick told Tom about the background …

"A colleague of mine, Chris Bull, ran a series of courses in ICI in 1972 that helped people think about their life and how they would like it to be. The heart of the course was Core Process work. I used Core Process to meet people's needs like career counselling and management development, but never in a very systematic or focussed way. It was just another tool in my toolkit."

Tom liked the sound of this and booked himself in, there and then, to 'get done'. A few weeks later, when Tom found out his Core Process was Breathing Life, it immediately led to Nick and Tom discussing how to maximise the potential of this tool. Tom pointed out that Nick could train people in the methodology and, in this way, many more people could benefit from learning their Core Process. Three months later, a business was formed, five new people, including Tom were trained in how to discover peoples' Core Process and the plans made to grow the business further in 2006, even taking it outside the UK.

In summary, Nick and Tom would simply never have met if it wasn't for on-line networking, serendipity and the ability to recognise coincidences and act upon them.

John Cave and Sam Thiara met as a result of a BRE breakfast. Sam runs a business that helps owner/managers of SMEs to grow their company, essentially business coaching. "I had no real interest in this, but enjoyed chatting to Sam and started getting to know a bit more about him and his background", notes John.

At the time, Sam was tasked by an Indian components manufacturer to open up a supply to NSK, one of the largest players in the automotive sector worldwide, in the UK. He managed this operation, including setting up the logistics, quality control and product sourcing. As a result of this work he developed a good number of contacts in India who are experts in this field.

John continues, "Sam was preparing a trip out to India, and mentioned that he was meeting these people, and asked if I needed him to look out for contacts for the logistics work that I am doing out there. We got chatting again, and the seeds of the business proposition popped into our heads simultaneously. We arranged a conference call while Sam was with his contacts to discuss fully with them, and it went very well. As a logistics company we have a number of customers in the engineering sector. This is a sector that is being squeezed at the moment due to the decline of manufacturing in the UK, and the rise of high-quality, low-cost imports. Many companies don't know what to do to establish a trusted relationship with a foreign partner".

Putting the two together, John and Sam are able to offer trusted partnerships between UK and Indian companies with quality control and assurance and a complete supply chain solution, using John's network in India and Europe to provide a no-hassle-door-to-door service. They also offer business experience in establishing these links and business coaching to make the most of the potential, avoiding the potential pitfalls of sourcing and supply.

In 2004, Luke Pittaway and Maxine Robertson of Lancaster University Management School produced a paper for UK Government called *Business to Business Networking and its Impact on Innovation: Exploring the UK Evidence*. The paper reflected the findings of a systematic literature review on networking and innovation. Their findings suggested that the diversity of collaborations between industries or between science and industry were found to provide a key source of innovation. Integrating suppliers during the early stages of product innovation was found to be essential for success and the role of customers early in the idea generation and development phase was confirmed. Third parties, like professional associations, acted as neutral knowledge brokers and conduits for the diffusion of innovation between firms. "As innovation has become more complex, networks begin to hold greater strategic significance. The studies reviewed show that alliance structures, management competencies and strategic network management have a bearing on the success of innovation within firms."

The paper explored the specific networking practices in the UK and explored its network infrastructure. From the empirical evidence the paper concludes that firms in the UK have relatively strong relationships with firms in their direct market (e.g. suppliers) and relationships between firms and science partners in the UK are considered to be strong comparatively to competitors. General weaknesses for UK firms revolve around the competencies of individuals and firms to leverage maximum value from networks. The overall networking infrastructure in the UK was found to be limited in a number of respects. Based on these findings it was concluded that in the UK networking did contribute to innovation and that UK employees and firms did engage with networks extensively.

With changes in corporate structure to focus on the core and the potential growth of 'outsourced innovation', the conclusion that "UK firms have tended to rely on the networking capabilities of too few individuals in their relationships with other firms and that contacts have been too short-term, being one-off and intermittent" should be of concern to business leaders. If innovation springs from smaller, more flexible units that are not surrounded by the red tape of modern reporting requirements, larger firms need to be networking actively to find the right combinations of firms to help them to innovate. Another finding – that too many relationships were based on personal ties that were lost if the individuals moved on – should also argue for consistency and stability in the networking relationships between firms.

In a Demos paper, Charles Leadbeater and Paul Miller, document a change that they are now seeing in the economy and across society. They call it the pro-am revolution and comment "The 20th century was shaped by the rise of professionals. But now a new breed of amateurs has emerged."

In an article in Fast Company in October 2004, Leadbetter notes "The 20th Century was marked by the rise of professionals in medicine, science, education and politics. In one field after another, amateurs and their ramshackle organisations were driven out by people who knew what they were doing and had certificates to prove it. Now that historic shift seems to be reversing. Even as large corporations extend their reach, we're witnessing the flowering of pro-am, bottom-up self organisation."

Leadbetter argues that rap music along with pro-am distribution such as Kazaa and Napster are evidence of this movement. LINUX, claim Leadbetter and Miller, is the product of mass participatory innovation among thousands of pro-am technologists. In the developing world the Grameen Bank, founded by Muhammad Yunus, a Bangladeshi economics professor, trains barefoot bankers to deliver loans to people earning less than a dollar a day. This pro-am workforce makes it possible to administer cost effectively 2.8 million loans worth more than $4 million.

Some professionals will find the Pro-Am movement unsettling and they will seek to defend their monopolies, suggests Leadbetter. "The more enlightened will understand that the landscape is changing. Knowledge is widely distributed, not controlled in a few ivory towers. The most powerful organisations will enable professionals and amateurs to combine distributed know-how to solve complex problems". Pro-Ams could fuel mass participation in formal politics and in social entrepreneurship, he suggests. "They will play important economic roles as co-producers of services and sources of ideas. Democracy will be livelier, innovation more vibrant, social capital stronger and individual well-being more securely grounded. After a century in decline, amateurs will rise again. And they will change the world".

Networks and Entrepreneurs

Entrepreneurs cannot exist in a vacuum. They may start with an idea but, in order for it to grow and thrive, they will need access to skills, to money, to advocates and, eventually, to customers. Indeed, in many ways, the customer is the first of these. Without a market, a lot of effort will be expended and a lot of money spent for no effect. A network of customers can give crucial answers early in the development cycle that may make the difference between success and failure.

In an article *Working the Net* in Entrepreneur magazine (July 2005), C. J. Prince notes that "Social networking sites offer entrepreneurs a chance to connect with investors, potential partners and customers". She quotes Paul Allen of Infobase as saying "The most important thing for an entrepreneur is not necessarily what they know, but who they know". Prince also points to Tim Connors, general partner at US venture partners and a co-founder of Spoke Software. Connors believes that virtual communities help small businesses find not just potential customers but also board members and other strategic business partners. The speed with which this can be done can have a direct impact on companies' success. "We need to get to companies quickly and understand quickly whether there was an opportunity there" Connors is quoted as saying.

Simon Rogers, an Ecademy member and entrepreneur, has been successful in building new businesses using networks both online and offline to grow them and to find the right connections. In an article on about.com, David Teten and Scott Allen note that he has uncovered over £1 million in potential revenues as a result of his participation in Ecademy. "After just four months in business, he has been introduced to more than 16 opportunities, each with £75,000 or more." In an interview for this book, Rogers points out that it is possible to find business through networking. In 2004, he opened a business from scratch with no pipeline and no marketing other than networking. After the first year the after-tax turnover was £80,000.

To make Global Labour Matching a reality, many more members of networks will need to innovate and then take their ideas to market. While networks can be seen as a pool of potential labour, there will also need to be innovation and entrepreneurship to succeed.

8 *Managing Networks*

M anagement is frequently driven from the top down through a hierarchy. There are line managers and the general flow of information is from bottom to top, stage by stage, and from top to bottom in the same way. Such approaches are called command and control.

Networks have no implied (or explicit) hierarchy. All relationships are peer-to-peer and information flows in many directions simultaneously. Unlike hierarchical systems, there can be no command-and-control in a network. Networks also exist in command and control environments, where their informal information flow may also be called the 'grapevine'. It is often more effective than the upwards and downwards flow of information around the hierarchy.

Online networks walk the line between permission and restriction. Some are more permissive than others. Content provided by members may be useful or self-serving, accurate or inaccurate, constructive or destructive, involving or offensive. Some content may be illegal in one or more countries where the network is present – or, indeed, as the Internet is global, where the network is not present. Determining what content is acceptable will always have some element of subjective judgement.

This dichotomy is not lost on the management team of Ecademy.

Glenn Watkins, Chief Executive, believes that you should let the network develop its own path. "Growth comes at the edges of the network where the members are active – let go and it will happen." That does not mean, he says, that Ecademy does not need to have rules for good behaviour and good practice on the network. "When growing a network, there will be people who wish to follow their own agenda. If this conflicts with that of the network and the majority of its members, action must be taken to deal with that." The steps taken will be different in each case but, from time to time, every network will find the need to remove content and/or members for the better functioning of the network for the majority.

Corporates, too, will find that giving freedom to employees, for example, to join social or business networks as representatives of their company or to blog in that capacity, places a responsibility on the employee to maintain the reputation of the firm. Sole traders and directors of smaller firms also risk their reputation (and that of their firm) by their behaviour and content on public fora of all types. Separating the personal you from the corporate you will be difficult, if not impossible, in a world where search engines record your every post.

The management of networks will find, as well, that their actions may have consequences that they must deal with. In the run-up to the Live8 concerts in July 2005, eBay had a number of Live8 tickets on offer from independent vendors. Those tickets had been allocated, free, in a ballot by the Live8 organisers. The community within eBay was outraged at the profiteering behaviour and directed their anger not just at the vendors but at eBay for allowing the offers to remain live. The speed and intensity of the reaction was remarkable and effective, as Wired magazine reported at the time:

> Tickets were allocated Monday via an SMS lottery. More than 2 million text messages were entered, at a cost of £1.50 ($2.70) each, to join the lottery for 133,000 tickets. Some winners

immediately listed tickets on eBay, and some sold for more than £2,000 ($3,600).

On Tuesday, outraged eBay members began flooding the ticket auctions with fake bids that drove prices up to £10 million ($18 million). The phoney bids made the sale of tickets impossible, as almost every bid was fraudulent. Some eBay members used their own accounts, possibly jeopardizing their hard-earned eBay ratings. Others opened new accounts to place fake bids, including one called live8legalteam, prompting speculation that the bidding was organized by Live8 itself.

eBay also came under fire from organizer Bob Geldof, a musician best known for his 1985 Live Aid African famine-relief benefit concert that raised more than $200 million. Geldof blasted eBay for allowing people to sell the free tickets. "What eBay are doing is profiteering on the backs of the impoverished," Geldof said in a statement quoted by Reuters.

On Tuesday, eBay banned all ticket sales.

"We have listened to eBay's community of users and the message has been clear – that they do not want the tickets to be resold on the site," said Doug McCallum, eBay managing director, in a statement. "Once we are made aware of any Live8 tickets being resold, they will be taken down."

This balance between the ownership of the network and their plans for growth and development and the needs and desires of the community as a whole, and of groups within it, is always present.

The danger of the network being hijacked by vocal members is always there, and managements respond in differing ways.

The bigger the network, the more investment there is in it by both members and management, and the greater the tendency towards dispute and disagreement. Ecademy has responded – like several other networks and discussion groups – by setting rules for behaviour and recruiting members to help work with the membership to ensure that rules are observed. Ecademy mentors provide this function.

Some claim that this breaches free speech and makes the network bland, others see immense benefits from having a safe place to network. It is difficult to see how the two views will be reconciled.

As big media continue to buy into the network community – News Corp and mySpace, ITV and Friends Reunited – it is interesting to watch how these top-down, broadcast media adapt to networked, interactive communities. Already, mySpace has been subject to complaints that members are being censored when they mention or link to a rival site.

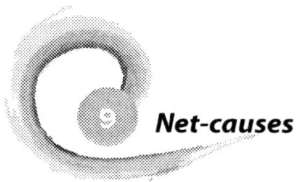 **Net-causes**

Communication through networks is essentially democratic. No one node has more authority or access than any other. Networks are conversation-based. So the information that passes across a network reflects face-to-face conversation and can be accurate or inaccurate, factual or propaganda. Causes of many kinds will use networks as their best way of developing a wider following. Causes such as charitable appeals, brand campaigns, single issue groups and terrorists will use the facilities of networks to spread their words and to grow and maintain their networks of followers.

Al Qaeda, responsible for 9/11 in the USA and bombings around the world including those in London, Madrid and Bali, is a network. Despite the frequent mentions of Osama bin Laden as its head, it appears to be an autonomous network where most groups (cells) decide on their own actions and take them, keeping others in the network informed.

Anti-globalisation supporters use message boards, web sites and SMS messaging to organise protests. Again, individual members or cells, choose to take action and post the information for others to see.

At the other end of the scale, networks were activated on December 26th 2005 to channel money and assistance into the countries affected by the Asian Tsunami. The response on Ecademy was instant and members donated over £13,000 to the Red Cross, whilst others made donations direct to other charities. Communication was established between people on the ground and concerned people on Ecademy throughout the duration of the emergency and its aftermath.

In 2003, Thomas worked with Malcolm McQuarrie on a concept which they called Routecause. It was based on the premise that businesses, especially the bigger brands, would be vulnerable to networked assaults on their reputation – something that now happens regularly. Routecause promoted the idea that companies need to network with their customers and listen and react to their needs and feedback. Brands will become causes in their own right to seek attention. This is more than just cause-related marketing or sponsorship and is likely to grow out of Corporate Social Responsibility (CSR). 2005 was the EU Year of CSR, so expect more traction toward Routecause after that.

In early 2006, a number of companies are beginning to embrace the Routecause philosophy. American Express have launched RED, a cause-related credit card, described as a "21st century idea" by Amex's Chief Marketing Officer, John Hayes. The idea came from Bono of the rock band U2 and a lobbyist for humanitarian action. According to Amex, RED is "something that will be good for the people of Africa, good for consumers and good for business." This is the type of win/win/win that is at the heart of Routecause.

Nestle now have a page dedicated to social responsibility on their website with policies and thinking around Africa and Infant Formula milk amongst other items. UK Retailer Marks and Spencer has launched a line of clothing made with Fairtrade cotton. Maybe Routecause's time has come?

The situation since 2003 has changed only in the accessibility of the means of publication by any aggrieved consumer and the speed with which a campaign can be mounted. An example might be the 'Dell Hell' campaign.

Web analysis company Onalytica, in a December, 2005 White Paper 'Measuring the Influence of Bloggers on Corporate Reputation' notes that, "In June, 2005, blogger Jeff Jarvis complained about his new Dell on his blog Buzzmachine. It appeared that despite his paying extra for the machine to be repaired by an engineer at his home, the company was not in fact able to provide this service" Not, on the face of it, a reason for Dell to be concerned. However, as Jarvis blogged about the problem, "he received hundreds and then thousands of links, emails and comments from other angry Dell customers. He became their spokesman." Onalytica continue the story: "Over the next few days and weeks, other aggrieved customers and interested bloggers discovered and responded to his problems. Dell responded to Jarvis by offering a refund. One of its spokespeople commented that the company had a 'look, don't touch' policy about blog commentary. In July 2005, Dell closed down their popular online customer service forum. Whether coincidentally or not, Dell's sales stalled."

Jarvis coined the term 'Dell Hell' and a Google search for that phrase on Google brings up Buzzmachine as the second entry. The top entry and several of the top ten are references to Jarvis' blog. The term 'Dell Customer Service' brings Dell's site back at the top but has many references to Jarvis' blog in the top 10. This is the power of one individual campaigning against a major organisation.

Asked about Jarvis' complaints by CRN Magazine in January, 2006, Michael Dell commented, "We don't want anyone to have a bad experience, whether they are a blogger or anyone else."

In a press release accompanying the White Paper, Flemming Madsen at Onalytica comments, "It's old news that pressure groups can inflict pain on sales and brand value. However, as the world has moved online, brand owners are likely to face more and more effective pressure from well-organised special interest groups. These pressure groups have significantly fewer resources than the brands they are trying to influence. However, when combining their cause with the nature of the online world and (typically) a better understanding of how the Internet and search engines work, they can often gain substantial influence on direct sales and long term brand value. Because the traditional barriers of entering the debate have been removed, brand owners need a wake up and understand how they can defend their brands effectively online or suffer the loss in brand value and sales."

On the face of it, online networks should be ideal places for MLM and Network Marketing to grow. However, many networks explicitly ban MLM/NM activity. Glenn Watkins explains why Ecademy follows that policy, "If each agent of an MLM scheme joins and starts approaching members to become part of their downline (members recruited from whom the recruiter earns commission), it creates a huge nuisance for members. Ecademy takes no action against members who properly advertise products or services but will actively discourage recruitment activity, to the point of removing the member in question."

In July 2005, the Live8 concert took place in a number of places simultaneously and was supported by an online petition to which viewers could add their details. Several million people signed the petition. On this occasion, an opportunity to create an instant network based around the cause of making poverty history was arguably missed. The future will be very different and causes will use the collection of details online to create an ongoing debate about the issues raised. The causes with the biggest networks will have tapped into network power.

It is our contention that networking – using the networks we've already talked about to develop a reputation and a network of advocates – will be an important skill for the 21st Century. For many of us, it will be THE key skill, yet it is little taught in the education system. No one network can provide for all of our needs, and our time is important. So how do we make the most of the opportunities and avoid the worst of the pitfalls? What are the skills and strategies needed to network successfully?

A good place to begin might be to determine why you are networking. Not everyone is doing this for the same reason. For most, it is probably about finding work – employment or freelance contracting – but it may also be to gain a higher profile within target markets, to find partners to develop a business, to acquire or share information, to develop a social network to balance out lone working or to support a cause. It may be about several of these.

In a blog on Ecademy, Life Member Bjørn Guldager of ProMinds in Denmark categorised networkers into five types:

- The negative type who really does not want to network at all. He may have a feeling that he is missing out by not networking, but really, his 'world of one' is quite big enough for him.

- The conservative type will network, but only with people where he has a long 'common story' e.g. members of the same club, or when sufficient trust has been built up over a long period of time. You cannot easily reach this person.

- The reactive type will be open to new proposals and indeed networking relationships, but will be selective and thus keep control over his network – and he doesn't expand it much on his own account.

- The proactive type actually 'crosses the comfort zone border' and goes out to develop the network in the way he wants, but is selective about the projects he dives into and the people he approaches. The focus is on quality, he prioritises his time and he takes responsibility for making it happen.

- The hyperactive type networks with anyone using any medium and believes strongly in quantity and possibly even 'random connections' as they may lead to something at some point. Quantity and energy are two characteristics but with less focus on priority.

Bjørn points out that no type is 'better' than the others, they are just different. "Once you've identified your main type (and often you'll be between two of them), what you can do is to try being 'the next type in the sequence'. A conservative networker will not be happy suddenly acting in a hyperactive way but may experiment with (reactively) accepting a few networking proposals, 'giving it a chance'. And the reactive networker may benefit from trying a few proactive stints out there.

We know that redundancy, unemployment and self employment will touch more people in the 21st Century as the world 'flattens' more, with more outsourcing and greater competition driving down prices. We believe there will be a growing need for more portfolio jobs.

If you aren't already networking, then you should start NOW.

Starting to network when you're out of work or when you urgently need to build a team is too late. You should be networking when you don't need to. That way your network will be active and supportive when you do need it.

People think networking is simple. You go to meetings, give people your business card, tell them what you do and you'll get business. We've heard variations on the theme many times. In our opinion, that view is just plain wrong. Look at it from a recipient's point of view. You're at a meeting and a person comes up to you, thrusts his business card at you and begins to sell. Are you going to buy? Unlikely. Who is he? How do we know if we can work with him? How does he know what he could do for us? What about that perfect customer that we have but will never tell him about because he never asked?

Networking is not selling. It is a stage before a sale is even possible. Networking is about two or more people getting to know each other. Getting to know each other, moreover, as people. This is scary territory for some of us. We have to connect as a human being not as a sales automaton. Only when we know each other better might there be a move to doing business. When you do know each other, trust begins to build and, when it reaches an appropriate level, you might place an order or recommend that another of your connections do so.

The process of networking is not linear. The chapters that follow don't prescribe any order of play other than the need to develop a profile that others can relate to early in the process. It won't be the profile you use once you've been networking a few months because the initial learning curve is steep and your emphasis will change.

Your Profile on networks is important. Profiles are living 'work in progress', just as people are.

Building a network takes time and care. There is a recurring debate about quality and quantity in networking which we will examine, along with tips and techniques for approaching potential connections.

Today's world is full of content. We are all publishers now. The tools are abundant and very available. But what should we say and where should we say it? We will look at the options and the potential of blogging and other content creation inside and outside of the networks.

Joining and being active in clubs will give you an opportunity to get to know people well. Clubs are the online way of building close relationships, and many offer a chance to meet your new friends and acquaintances at events. Starting and running a club is good for your reputation and allows you to demonstrate your expertise. We see the potential for the YOU club, a club based around you and your interests, as a way of delivering your products or ser-vices to an audience. You choose whether to charge or not but chargeable clubs will become a feature of 21st Century business.

In his 2003 book, 'Networking for Life', Thomas set out 10 networking 'commandments'. As most of them are still relevant, we have included them in Appendix 1.

Your profile tells people who you are, what you stand for and what you can do to help others. It should be an introduction to you and provide hooks that others can use to connect to you. It is not your CV, though it may contain some elements of that. It is more rounded – more about the real you.

Reputation takes a long time to build and can be destroyed in an instant. It can also mature and develop even after we die. Not everyone we posthumously recognise as important or interesting was famous in their lifetime, and not everyone who was famous in their lifetime is now remembered. Thomas Power says "I've always been told by people that you're not immortal. When you die, you die and you're gone. But we still talk about Jesus. We talk about Reubens, Rembrandt, John D Rockefeller. We still talk about people because of their reputation. I'm much more interested in my repu-tation than I am in money, much more interested in relationships than I am in money."

How does this affect the way you might go about developing your profile on Ecademy? Thomas always tries to encourage people to make their profile their reputation, a reflection of their whole life past, present and future. Since the start of Ecademy in 1998, three members who Thomas knew personally have died "and their profiles don't reflect what they've achieved in their lives. I think that your profile should reflect what you've achieved and what you're trying to achieve, why you're in this community, what you're giving to the community, what you hope to get from this community. It's not just a display of your expertise."

Thomas thinks your profile should be immortal. His profile has been written as if he is dead which spooks some people. Thomas understands that, but "I want people to read it and know that I tried to make a contribution. I think your profile should say that. These computer systems allow us to record history. Blogging is live history. Google remembers you forever." Your profile is your imprint on the planet – whether you put your profile on Ecademy or on another network.

We have already established that, to be successful in the 21st Century work environment, we will need to take control of the management of our personal brand and of our reputation. We all have a personal brand – even those of us in employment – it's just that some of us don't manage it actively, and we all have a reputation. Your brand is what you say you do and your reputation is built by the actions you take. They are different but need to be congruent. We will have to market ourselves.

Philip Kotler, in his classic 'Principles of Marketing', talks about the four Ps of Marketing

- Product
- Price
- Promotion
- Place

If you and what you can offer are the Product, then you will need to establish how you price your services. We can see a change developing where more professionals and tradespeople will charge for their services through Chargeable Clubs with a monthly fee for access to your services, expertise or information.

Promotion in an online environment is about the content you create and to which you contribute. You do need to consider both the quality and consistency of the content alongside your brand and reputation, and the Place where the promotion will happen.

To be seen and discovered in the online world, you need to feature high on the rankings of the main search providers – Google, Yahoo and MSN. None of these sites directly publish content, so you will need to find search engine-friendly places to execute your marketing plans.

The major social and business networks seem to be the right places for this to happen. As do blogging sites like Blogger, Wordpress and Typepad. Consolidators like Technorati, Bloglines and Squidoo will also provide suitable places to add content.

In putting content together, it is crucial to know what your customers or collaborators might be looking for and to be very aware that all of your web-based content is viewable (and virtually unerasable).

As we point out in a later chapter, blogs work best if they provide added value and interest, and least well as full-on advertising. There is a skill in getting this right, whilst ensuring that your keywords (as seen by a searcher) get picked up in Google and the other Search Sites.

Some sites let you advertise instead of or as well as blogging. Craigslist, eBay and Ecademy all allow advertising. How you operate in those places should be consistent with the content you blog and should match your brand and reputation.

On Ecademy, blogging and 'flogging' (i.e. advertising) are now alongside each other on the Home Page – a recognition that both approaches have their place in the marketing mix, and often work in tandem. Creating a blog and a 'flog' at the same time gets twice the chance of being picked up by casual readers.

In the 1970s, a fifth P was added – People. Whilst the networks are Places, the People in them are of great interest. These are the people who will support and guide you, help you improve your arguments and proposition, introduce you to suitable prospects, operate as your advocates and, from time to time, be your customers. If you have this wider vision, you will find the right people to help you.

When networking, it is important to tune into opportunities. As you listen – and you should be listening more than you are talking – you should be searching for the keywords. These will show how you can help the person you're listening to, either directly or by connecting them with people or resources that can help them.

Different networks have different approaches to profiles. LinkedIn for example, has a very businesslike approach with current, former jobs and roles prominent. That fits with LinkedIn's view of the networking world – a directory for connecting with people where most of the follow-up will be elsewhere. There are tools on LinkedIn to allow you to enter keywords and to search on them, and the ability to email your contacts to notify an update of your profile (which people use for a variety of purposes). This shows a recognition of the need to use the platform for maintaining connections. LinkedIn, as yet, has no facility to add a photograph.

Networks with a more social element – Ecademy, openBC, Ryze, Soflow and others – have more tools for maintaining contacts, including private messages and active clubs. They also allow more informal contacts. In LinkedIn, all connections between people who don't already know each other must be 'brokered' by mutual contacts. The other networks encourage approaches to members based only upon their profile, and many strong connections have started this way. The more hooks you create, the more likely it is that others will connect with you.

So what are the hooks? Ecademy Profiles offer four options
- Your photograph
- Your 50 words i.e. keywords
- Your profile text
- Marketplace entries

The importance of the photograph cannot be overestimated. People buy from people they like and trust, and liking can be quickly judged (rightly or wrongly) by your photograph. We all make instant judgements of people all the time, and face/appearance is critical to this process.

In the BBC TV programme 'How Art Made the World', Cambridge academic and presenter Nigel Spivey talks about the cult of personality that was used by Alexander the Great to keep control of the vast Macedonian empire. His face, in stylised form, really was his brand. In his book of the TV programme, Spivey describes how the tomb of Alexander's father Philip was found to contain an interesting artefact, "…a number of carved heads and bodies were perceived to be, on closer inspection, part of a lively hunting scene along one side of the couch. Small as they were ... these heads were nonetheless very individualised – and at least one of the young hunters on horseback had to be Alexander. An arched brow, an upward, 'melting' gaze, the neck distinctly tilted: these were unmistakable characteristics of the man as described by ancient writers and captured by ancient artists." Philip died in 336 BC so the likenesses were from that year or earlier. The importance of the find? "This was the image that would serve Alexander throughout his brief life, and forever after."

Spivey speculates on the involvement of Aristotle in the image-making of Alexander. "The subject of physiognomics is among his recorded scientific interests. For him, physical attributes, especially facial features, carried strong indications of personality." Image was a "matter of concern" to Alexander. His biographer, Plutarch, notes Spivey, "explicitly tells us that Alexander maintained in his entourage three image specialists, each outstanding in his medium – whether sculpture (Lysippus), painting (Apelles), or gem-cutting (Pyrogoteles). This third artist may have been responsible for encapsulating Alexander's look numismatically, for, like Darius before him, Alexander realised that spreading a message by coinage was highly effective – even in parts of his empire (such as Arachosia, in modern Afghanistan) where coins served no daily economic function."

As part of the programme, psychologist Stian Reimers of the University of Warwick devised an experiment to show the importance of face. He created two manifestos, one with a face more prominent than a logo, the other with the logo more prominent. Stian comments: "The 100-participant experiment itself was run online, which let me counterbalance the text and layout on the two posters – something that isn't possible in a real election campaign. There were two layouts and sets of text: Version A and Version B. Half of the participants saw Face-Version A/Logo-Version B and the other half saw Logo-Version A/Face-Version B. Basically it was a pretty small, but significant, effect in the experiment – people preferred the face to the logo. Clearly, with an experiment of this design we can't generalise to all posters with faces being better than all posters without."

Reimers comments that "Overall, the consensus seems to be that a good face will encourage trust and compliance more than a good logo, and the experiment I ran supported this view. That said, there's not a lot of research on the topic". In American research presented in 1987 under the title 'The Image and the Vote – Manipulating Voters' Preferences', Shawn W. Rosenberg and Patrick McCafferty of the University of California examined "the ability of campaign consultants to shape candidates' images", specifically concentrating on non-verbal aspects. They conclude: "Using photographs, we demonstrated that different presentations of the same person could produce quite different images of that person's likeableness, integrity, competence and general fitness for public office. This suggests that, with appropriate pretesting and adequate control over a candidate's public appearance, a campaign consultant should be able to significantly manipulate the image projected to the voting public".

In the online world, photographs on profiles also make a difference to perceptions of a person's likeableness, integrity and competence. The more attractive the image, the more visitors and page hits that individual receives.

Keywords are also important hooks. In both Ecademy (your 50 words) and LinkedIn, they are hyperlinked to find other people who have the same keywords. Ecademy also allows you to search for 'people like me' based on the 50 words. Keywords are your choice but should be about you as an individual as well as your work persona. People first connect at a personal level when given a choice.

The free text profile should also give hooks. The first paragraph is used by Google as explanatory text. Use it to summarise who you are, using keywords and phrases with which you would expect people to search for you. Then state who you are, what you stand for and what you do – in that order. Give the profile plenty of thought and keep that and your 50 words changing through time to retain interest. Remember to be focused on the reader, and not the writer. Even though the profile is your selling tool, remember that people prefer to buy rather than be sold to. Provide enough attraction by being open and giving, and the interest will build. Remember to include hooks that will create action in the reader.

You only get one chance to make a good first impression. Make sure your profile tells people about you in the best way possible and make a great first impression.

Trust

It is a short word, only five letters, but the meaning of the word is so important. We only do business where we feel that we have enough assurance or trust that the risks are worth accepting. When we choose to do business with someone, we first do a risk assessment. It may be done unconsciously, for example when we buy a newspaper, based on recognition of the brand and on the relatively small risk being taken, or it may be a real exercise, for example when choosing a new IT system. This may involve extensive research and due diligence. Trust is relative to the risk and the value of the task in hand. I might trust my newsagent to sell me a newspaper or magazine, but not a diamond ring. There are many factors involved in creating trust, and these will be made more complex if the relationship is online rather than offline.

When we are online, we often use triangles of trust, though we may not always recognise them as such. On a simple level, paying by credit card gives you a trust triangle with the merchant and your credit card company. You trust the credit card company, and therefore you trust the merchant – in a lot of cases it is unnecessary to trust the merchant, as the credit card company will make a full restitution of any loss in the transaction. The credit card company is trusted because there is a relationship between your bank, yourself and the credit card company. Groups like Mastercard and Visa also add trust to the process by building trusted branding. So it is when dealing with online merchants like eBay. We trust eBay, so if eBay trusts the seller, we will buy from them with more confidence. The higher the value or the greater the risk, the more we may wish add our own risk assessment to that of eBay as – effectively – a Trusted Third Party.

Trusted third parties exist everywhere in the trust world. They may be banks or insurance companies, solicitors or accountants. Online they may also be service providers, like an ISP, or companies such as eBay or Amazon, who are held in good repute.

Social networks create trust relationships between members. LinkedIn uses members to broker introductions. It is the trust between the requesting member and the forwarding member that makes it possible for the target member to accept a trusted connection. Ecademy uses a rating system, not scientific but none the less indicative, to give some clarity on who it is possible to trust. Testimonials also help. The final step is almost always a face-to-face meeting if the value/risk of the transaction demands it or, if that is not possible, a telephone or video-conference. It is said that eBay's acquisition of Skype for $4.2 billion in 2005 was to make it easier for buyers and sellers across the world to communicate with each other during the bidding process. Some of the valuation also reflected the 'stored up revenue' inside Skype's payment collection system.

Reputation

Your reputation will build in many ways from your content, but much more from your actions. As you develop a network of people and give to them as they need, some will be moved to provide the ultimate in reputation builders – a testimonial. LinkedIn and Ecademy have specific places for testimonials to be added. Don't ask for them, nor expect people to give them – but do give them as often as you feel they are merited, and be very specific. 'Thomas is a great guy', whilst true, is too general for most purposes. 'Penny helped me to understand what my real passion is and I'm doing more business and enjoying myself more' is much more specific and will contribute to the strength of the triangle of trust. Testify to their actions more than their attributes and that will be a powerful give indeed. Do that and your own testimonials will also build.

So who are you?

For many people, writing their profile is a cathartic process. It is only at this stage that they may realise that 'who they are' is not necessarily 'who they were'. Simply trying to encapsulate who we are can be a trigger for further investigation. It is crucial to know who we are.

If we don't know who we are, how can we expect others we meet to know? People buy from people they like and trust and every move we make, every word we speak sends messages to others about our attitude, beliefs and trustworthiness.

Your success in business will be, at least partially, dependant upon how people perceive you. We are not suggesting that you fake sincerity or try to change yourself into a better person, whatever that is. What we are suggesting is that, in order to brand yourself, you first need to understand yourself.

The Johari window is a concept used by Human Resources professionals and therapists to explain why, sometimes, people see a different you to the one you see. The window is divided into four, usually unequal sized, panes which represent four aspects of you.

- **The Public You**
  That part of you that is known to you and to the other person. This will differ person to person.

- **The Private You**
  That part of you that you know but keep hidden from the other person.

- **The Revealed You**
  That part of you that others see but you cannot.

- **The Hidden You**
  The part of you that is unknown to you AND to the other person. It is often revealed in stressful situations as it was in the case of Sandy Nininger, which we report in the next Chapter.

These panes can be changed in size by two actions:

- **Intimacy (into-me-see)** – allows the other person to see more of the Private you. By doing this, you create the beginnings of trust. That may be built by further revelations from both parties.

- **Feedback** – allows you to see how the other person sees you and to choose whether to act differently as a result. Formal feedback (as in a review or appraisal) is useful but many people miss the signs of informal feedback which may come from the words and actions of the other person. Listening well and reading body language accurately are important assets for a good networker.

There is a constant flow of intimacy and feedback happening in every friendship. The more people know about you, the more they see are able to make judgements about trusting you. The more you know about yourself, the more you can do to correct unfortunate characteristics that reduce your attractiveness and accentuate the more positive parts of you.

It is our firm belief that, to survive and prosper in the new world of work and business, you will need to reveal yourself for who you truly are. There will be some who seek to exploit this but more will respect your open approach.

W̶e are all different and that difference is important. Nevertheless, there are times when we need to categorise people. When we come to build teams or work with others, there may be particular characteristics we need to find or roles we need to fill. Instinct helps, to a limited extent, when we interact with people face-to-face over a longer time but how can we get a shortcut to put over our strengths and our attributes quickly online?

For many of us, the answer lies in a number of profiling tools that, generally through questions and answers, identify characteristics which can be shared in a common language. These profiles are not you, they are simply a shorthand way of identifying a likely match to someone's needs. They may also be a way in which we can understand our own characteristics.

These profiles come from different approaches and can give entirely different insights. Some have become almost ends in themselves but, in general, they are just a means to achieve an end.

Some, like the Graves Spiral, represent our life developmental stage. Core Process gives insights into how we see and process the world, whilst personality tests like Myers Briggs, Enneagrams and Wealth Dynamics allow people to predict how we might relate to others and where we might fit into teams.

In a comprehensive article in the New Yorker magazine on September 20th 2004, Malcolm Gladwell (author of *Tipping Point* and *Blink*) analyses the personality testing phenomenon. In doing so he cites the case of Alexander (Sandy) Nininger, a quiet 23-year-old Lieutenant in the US Army serving in the Pacific in 1942. Nininger set off on a one-man mission to engage the enemy. He killed a number of enemy soldiers in his advance before he, himself, was killed. His Medal of Honor was the first of World War II. Gladwell writes, "Suppose that you were a senior Army officer…and were trying to put together a crack team of fearless and ferocious fighters. Sandy Nininger, it now appears, had exactly the right kind of personality for that assignment, but is there any way you could have known this beforehand? It clearly wouldn't have helped to ask Nininger if he was fearless and ferocious, because he didn't know that he was fearless and ferocious. His friends would have told you only that Nininger was quiet and thoughtful and loved the theatre …" Gladwell then examines the tests (and devises one of his own, a variation on MBTI) but has to conclude that after testing, "We will know all kinds of things about him, then. His personnel file will be as thick as a phone book, and we can consult our findings whenever we make decisions about his future. We just have to acknowledge that his file will tell us little about the thing we're most interested in. For that, we have to join him in the jungles of Bataan".

Finding your Emotional Wealth

In her blog on Emotional Wealth, Penny offered a framework for uncovering your route to Emotional Wealth.

> *Ask yourself these questions. Scribble them down on a big piece of paper, mind map them, draw them, – capture these thoughts however you want to:*
>
> 1. *Start with what you do now. This is your comfort zone and you know this so well.*
> 2. *Ask yourself: "How does this help others?"*
> 3. *Now, what is the reason you do it?*

4. *What difference does knowing you make to others?*

5. *What is your life journey that led you to where you are now?*

6. *How can you relate your present to your past?*

Now, write this up as a story.

1. *Write your journey.*

2. *Explain your purpose.*

3. *Tell me why you are passionate about your purpose.*

4. *Tell me why you are thrilled that you have the opportunity to fulfil your passion each day.*

5. *Tell me how you make this happen each day.*

6. *Tell me the difference you make to your clients.*

7. *Tell me exactly what you do.*

You have now identified your Emotional Wealth Value.

Having connected with your Emotional Wealth, you can use it to make your Profile more personal, to introduce yourself to people and to connect with your purpose whilst developing your business.

Core Process

Core Process is another way of determining your purpose and connecting with it. The story of how Tom Evans met Nick Heap and recognized the potential in Core Process is told in an earlier chapter.

That meeting led to the formation of the Flame Institute (http://www.theflameinstitute.com) which exists to develop practitioners and to help people find their 'flame'. "We believe that everyone has a 'Flame', a unique central strength and purpose. When you are using your flame, everything goes well. The Flame Institute's mission is to help people to discover their flame and use it to change the world for the better".

The process starts from the belief that everybody has a positive core that is unique. You have a unique strength, gift, purpose and passion – your Core Process. When you are using this fully, everything goes wonderfully well.

"So one way to happiness and fulfilment is to discover what your Core Process is," Tom Evans notes. "Luckily, this is simple, if not easy. It is also extraordinarily rewarding to help someone find his or hers."

The Core Process is a pair of words that capture the essence of you at your best. For Penny those words are 'Connecting Hearts' evidenced by her interest in Emotional Wealth and 'connecting your heart to your head'. 'Changing Lives' is apt for Thomas, who does so on a daily basis. They work well together, Connecting Hearts and Changing Lives, as a mission statement for all that Penny and Thomas do. Andy Coote's Core Process 'Leading the Way' has acted as a catalyst for him. Through illness, and also losing his way, he had stopped doing the things that were part of his Core Process. Leading the Way is truly who he is, but not what he was doing. For all of us, those words, and the process of reaching them, resonated strongly. It was an emotional activity and a process of change and, more importantly, understanding began from those sessions.

The Personal Development Spiral

Professor Clare Graves, a contemporary of Abraham Maslow, developed the 'Graves Spiral' in the early 20th Century as a way to represent the development of human thought over the centuries. It is, in the words of Ken Wilber, a 'holarchy' in which each level of the Spiral contains all of the lower levels.

According to Dr Don Beck, who has developed Spiral Dynamics (SD) from the research of the late Professor Graves, "The concept of Spiral Dynamics is that human nature is not fixed; we're not set at birth. Rather, we have the capacities, in the nature of the mind/brain itself, to construct new conceptual worlds. So what we are trying to describe is simply how humans are able, when things get bad enough, to adapt to their situation by creating greater complexities of thinking to handle new problems".

The Graves Spiral consists of eight levels of development in two tiers of what have become known as ᵛ*memes*.

Wikipedia notes "The term meme (from the Greek word mimema for 'something imitated') first came into popular use with the publication of the book *The Selfish Gene* by Richard Dawkins in 1976. The conceptual framework of memes borrows from the study of genes – the units of biological transmission. Different definitions of meme generally agree, very roughly, that a meme consists of some sort of a self-propagating unit of cultural evolution having a resemblance to the gene (the unit of genetics). Dawkins introduced the term after writing that evolution depended not on the particular chemical basis of genetics, but only on the existence of a self-replicating unit of transmission – in the case of biological evolution, the gene. For Dawkins, the meme exemplifies another self-replicating unit, and most importantly, one which he thought would prove useful in explaining human behavior and cultural evolution." Wikipedia, in its entry for Spiral Dynamics further adds that "the prepended and superscripted letter v indicates these are not basic memes but value systems which include them".

The ᵛmemes in the Graves spiral begin with the instinctive/survivalistic meme and ascend through magical/animistic, powerful/authoritarian, purposeful/meaningful and achievist/strategic to the top of the first-tier, communitarian/egalitarian. These first six ᵛmemes are defined as subsistence memes. Above them are the 'integrative' 'holistic' ᵛmemes.

The Graves Spiral has been developed by Dr Beck, who has added colours to the ᵛmemes for easier recognition, and by Dudley Lynch (author of the 1989 book, *The Strategy of the Dolphin*) who has concentrated on the triggers that move people from one level to the next. The colours used by Beck are:

- instinctive/survivalistic (beige)
- magical/animistic (purple)
- powerful/authoritarian (red)
- purposeful/meaningful (blue)
- achievist/strategic (orange)
- communitarian/egalitarian (green)
- integrative (yellow)
- holistic (turquoise)

Turquoise may not be the end of the story. Spiral Dynamics levels are reached by crises that demand new levels of thinking. A level above turquoise – being called Coral – is being talked about.

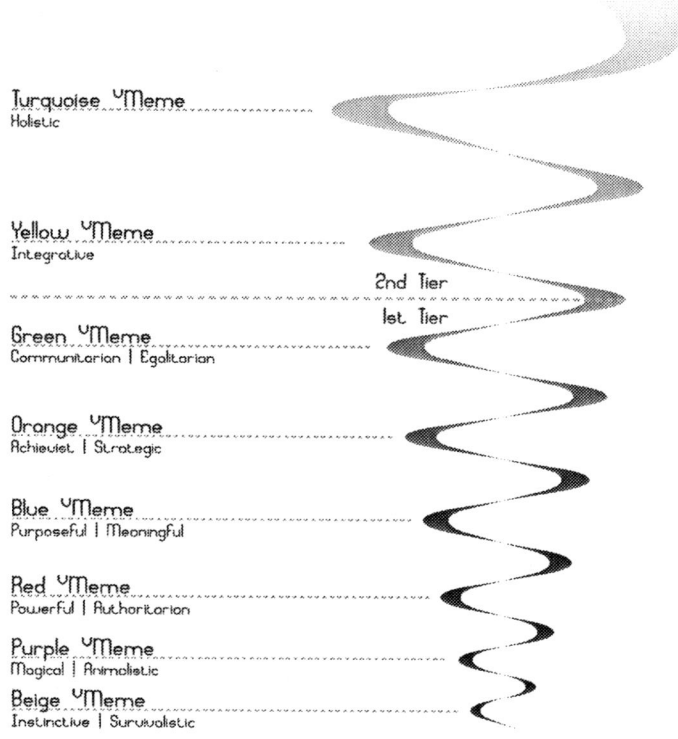

Turquoise ᵛMeme
Holistic

Yellow ᵛMeme
Integrative

2nd Tier

1st Tier

Green ᵛMeme
Communitarian | Egalitarian

Orange ᵛMeme
Achievist | Strategic

Blue ᵛMeme
Purposeful | Meaningful

Red ᵛMeme
Powerful | Authoritarian

Purple ᵛMeme
Magical | Animalistic

Beige ᵛMeme
Instinctive | Survivalistic

Dr Beck notes: "Spiral Dynamics is based on the assumption that we have adaptive intelligences "complex, adaptive, contextual intelligences, which develop in response to our life circumstances and challenges – what Spiral Dynamics calls Life Conditions. Like genes, viruses and bacteria, memes respond to the same basic principle in the universe, which is the concept of renewal, this regenerating capacity. Each successive meme contains a more expansive horizon, a more complex organising principle, with newly calibrated priorities, mindsets, and specific bottom lines. It's a way of solving problems. It's a way of assigning priorities to what's most important and why, formed in response to the life conditions."

Where an individual is placed on the spiral may be an inexact science. It is possible, in fact likely, that they will be exhibiting the characteristics of several levels simultaneously. Wilber, in his book *A Theory of Everything* (TOE), talks of aspects of us which he refers to as streams potentially being at their own levels of the spiral, such as cognition, morality, psychosexuality, role-taking, creativity and spirituality. A more complete list appears in TOE page 44.

Groupings, such as networks, can also have a place on the spiral based on their activity and outlook. In a blog on the subject on Ecademy in late 2005, there were a number of takes on where the network currently sits. A consensus settled on orange with elements of blue and green. Some aspects of the network might already be yellow. The ideals of the network suggest that a more yellow positioning will emerge with aspects of green, orange and blue still remaining. The move from green (which is 'pluralistic') to yellow (which is 'holistic') is described by Beck as a 'huge leap'. It may only happen when online networks work together as a whole. Now they are talking about being co-operative, but the reality of their co-operation is still some way off.

SD practitioners point out that "higher is not necessarily better" and that we all need to retain and use some elements of the 'lower' levels in order to survive.

Strength Finder

The book *Now Discover your Strengths* by Marcus Buckingham and Donald O. Clifton introduced the strength finder test. Inside the book is a ticket number that is entered to begin an online test. Characteristics with names like maximiser, learner, input, empathy, developer and relator are identified and your top five are produced as a report from the system. For example, Thomas' five attributes are WOO (Winning Others Over), Maximiser, Learner, Achiever and Command whilst Andy has Strategic, Input, Empathy, Futuristic and Maximiser. The idea is to cover as many types as possible within the team.

Belbin Team Role Model

The Belbin team role model concept was developed, over nine years to 1981, at Henley Management College by Dr Meredith Belbin and his team. It is based on a study of psychometrically tested managers across a variety of tasks in differing team compositions. The concept was first published by Dr Belbin in the book 'Management Teams – Why They Succeed or Fail'.

The Belbin website at www.Belbin.com identifies nine roles as follows:

- action-oriented roles – Shaper, Implementer, and Completer/ Finisher
- people-oriented roles – Co-ordinator, Teamworker and Resource Investigator
- cerebral roles – Plant, Monitor/Evaluator and Specialist.

The site goes on to comment: "Results from this research showed that there are a finite number of behaviours or TEAM ROLES that comprise certain patterns of behaviour which can be adopted naturally by the various personality types found among people at work. The accurate delineation of these TEAM ROLES is critical in understanding the dynamics of any management or work team".

You can get your Belbin team role assessment online at www. Belbin.com for a fee, as we write, of £25 per person.

Enneagrams

Enneagrams result from a simple test online that produces a percentage score across a number of possible types. Developed by Don Richard Russo and Ross Hudson, Enneagrams also have nine types, in this case arranged around the circle and with some types connected to others by lines within the circle.

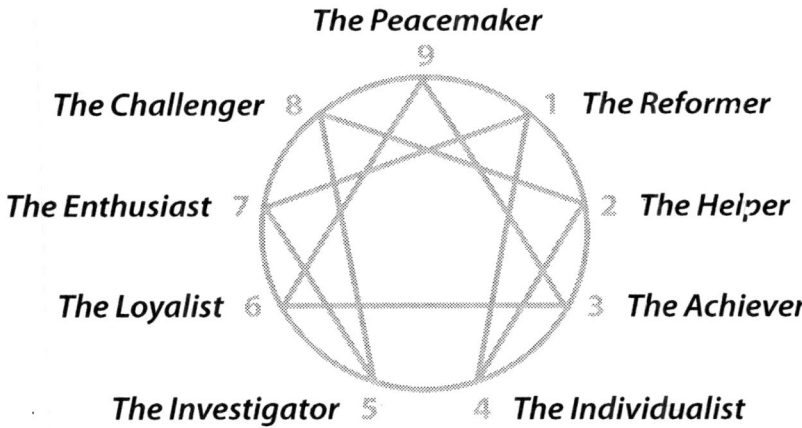

The Peacemaker
9

The Challenger 8   1 **The Reformer**

The Enthusiast 7   2 **The Helper**

The Loyalist 6   3 **The Achiever**

The Investigator 5   4 **The Individualist**

Although you may "find a little of yourself in all nine of the types" as the website www.enneagraminstitute.com notes, "one of them will stand out as being closest to yourself. This is your basic personality type". These personality types are influenced, according to the major Enneagram authors, by factors of inheritance and childhood, and we come into adulthood with our personality type fully formed. What's more, "people do not change from one basic personality type to another."

The types are also segmented into three triads (below, left) and each of these three triads have emotions attached to them (below, right).

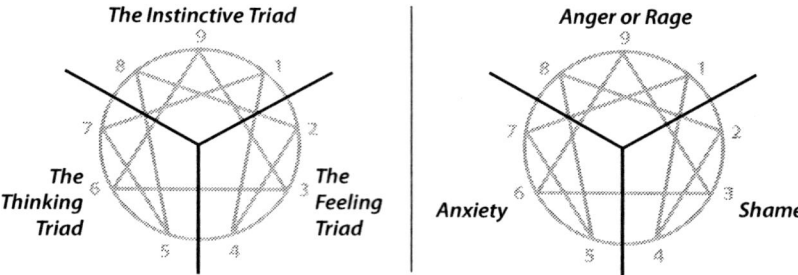

There is a wealth of detail on the website as well as the option to take a free assessment test. Andy's assessment as Number Four – "The Individualist" – described as "the sensitive, withdrawn type: expressive, dramatic, self-absorbed and temperamental" – is spot on the money.

Carl Jung and Personality Types

The next two personality typing systems owe a debt of gratitude to the works of Carl Jung (1875 - 1961) and to his work on personality. MBTI and Wealth Dynamics explicitly acknowledge Jung as a major influence.

Jung was the first to distinguish between introversion and extroversion. In his definition, introverts are people who prefer their internal world of thoughts, feelings, fantasies and dreams whilst extroverts prefer the external world of things and people and activities. Dr C. George Boeree notes in a paper about Jung (www.ship.edu/~cgboeree/jung.html) "The words have become confused with ideas like shyness and sociability, partially because introverts tend to be shy and extroverts tend to be sociable. But Jung intended for them to refer more to whether you (your 'ego') more often faced toward the persona and outer reality, or toward the collective unconscious and its archetypes. In that sense, the introvert is somewhat more mature than the extrovert. Our culture, of course, values the extrovert much more. And Jung warned that we all tend to value our own type most!"

Jung also identified four basic ways, or functions, in which we deal with the world both internally and externally. These are sensing, thinking, intuiting and feeling. Boeree, in his paper, describes them as follows:

Sensing means what it says: getting information by means of the senses. A sensing person is good at looking and listening and generally getting to know the world. Jung called this one of the irrational functions, meaning that it involved perception rather than judging of information.

Thinking means evaluating information or ideas rationally, logically. Jung called this a rational function, meaning that it involves decision making or judging, rather than simple intake of information.

Intuiting is a kind of perception that works outside of the usual conscious processes. It is irrational or perceptual, like sensing, but comes from the complex integration of large amounts of information, rather than simple seeing or hearing. Jung said it was like seeing around corners.

Feeling, like thinking, is a matter of evaluating information, this time by weighing one's overall, emotional response. Jung calls it rational, obviously not in the usual sense of the word.

All of these functions exist in each of us but in a sort of a league table from the superior function through secondary and tertiary functions to the inferior function.

Myers Briggs Type Indicator
Katharine Briggs and Isabel Briggs Myers developed this analysis based on Carl Jung's personality types work. It is widely used around the world to give a shorthand representation of the more prominent of four pairs of characteristics. These are:

Introvert/Extrovert	–	I/E
Intuitive/Sensing	–	N/S
Thinking/Feeling	–	T/F
Judging/Perceiving	–	J/P

These four character types produce 16 composite types (with names like ENFJ) which are determined by a balanced set of questions. Dr Boeree, in his article about Jung, says "What type you are says quite a bit about you – your likes and dislikes, your likely career choices, your compatibility with others, and so on. People tend to like it quite a bit. It has the unusual quality among personality tests of not being too judgemental: none of the types is terribly negative, nor are any overly positive. Rather than assessing how 'crazy' you are, the Myers Briggs simply opens up your personality for explanation".

Andy's INFP shows a bias towards introversion, intuition, feeling and perceiving. Thomas' ENFP shows a bias towards extravert (anyone who knows him well will attest to this) but otherwise a very similar profile. Penny's ESFJ shows a tendency towards sensing over intuition and judging over perceiving. It is important to remember that all of these classifications are based on a tendency towards one or other of the pair choices and that there will be elements of both in most people.

Some examples of MBTI profiles from the authors and Ecademy team:

Penny	–	ESFJ	–	Care Giver/Coach
Glenn	–	ENFJ	–	The Giver/Coach
Thomas	–	ENFP	–	Explorer/Inspirer
Julian Bond	–	INTP	–	Scientist/Thinker
Andy	–	INFP	–	Campaigner/Idealist

Myers Briggs type analysis is carried out by trained interviewers who can also provide context for the results and explain what can and can't be determined by them. There are also MBTI questionnaires on the Web which only ask a subset of the questions, and should be used with care.

Wealth Dynamics

A t the core of Wealth Dynamics, developed by Roger Hamilton and embodied in his XL results foundation, is a set of eight Wealth profiles. Like MBTI, these profiles have elements of Carl Jung's personality types, but also draw on the traditional Chinese I Ching which was brought to the west by Carl Jung. Roger brings together eastern and western thinking in this approach to building complementary, mutually supportive teams.

I Ching (Book of Changes) is, according to online encyclopedia Wikipedia "the oldest of the Chinese classic texts. It describes an ancient system of cosmology and philosophy which is at the heart of Chinese cultural beliefs. The philosophy centers on the ideas of the dynamic balance of opposites, the evolution of events as a process, and acceptance of the inevitability of change. In Western cultures, the I Ching is regarded by some as simply a system of divination; others believe it expresses the wisdom and philosophy of ancient China."

All Ecademy Life members (BlackStars) take the Wealth dynamics test as part of their induction and use the profile when putting together balanced teams. Ecademy has embraced the Wealth Dynamics system and now has representation of each Wealth Profile in its management team.

The eight profiles are arranged around a square as follows:

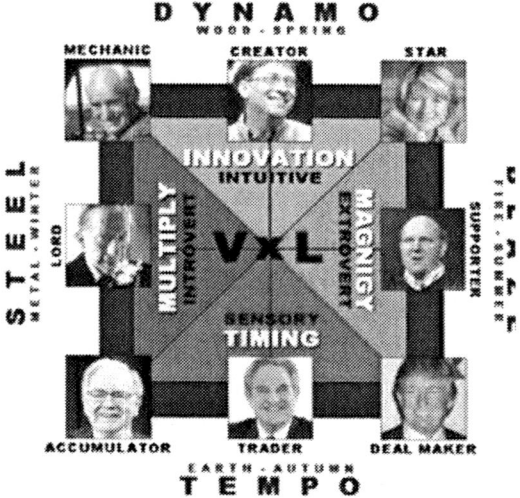

Each side of the square represents a season and an energy. At the top (mechanic—creator—star) we have spring and wood energy. And then clockwise we have summer and (hot) fire (star—supporter—dealmaker), autumn and earth (dealmaker—Trader—accumulator) and winter with (cold) steel (accumulator—lord—mechanic). This is a natural cycle from ideas to action to cash flow. Businesses and the industries that contain them move from spring and creation, through summer success into autumn decline and winter demise. The best, recognising this, find new 'springs' in order to create a whole new cycle before the first has run its course.

How would you recognise the types? We are grateful to Roger Hamilton for the following definitions.

The Creator

The Creator comes in two forms. The introverted Creator is an inventor: creative, artistic, and able to multi-task on many new ideas at the same time. The extroverted Creator is a pioneer: innovative but focused, creating not just products, but the businesses and marketing plans that will drive those products to market. Both are visionaries and motivate others by their drive.

Creator Role Models

Successful introverted Creators can be found most visibly in the design, media and entertainment industries. They are also behind every new and innovative product that reaches the market, from the most recent high-tech phone to the latest kitchen blender. Successful extroverted Creators are behind many start-ups and can be found at the head of high growth companies in high growth industries that require constant innovation to compete.

The highest profile Creators out there include Bill Gates, Steve Jobs and Larry Ellison on the one hand, and George Lucas, Steven Spielberg and Norman Foster on the other.

The Star

The Star has natural talent that others notice when it is shown. A unique personality and attributes are reason enough for people to talk about a Star. Naturally extroverted, Stars will be happy around others and will be quite comfortable being the centre of attention. As they also think more intuitively, they will have the ability to create the identity that suits them best.

Star Role Models

Stars, naturally, are the easiest of the profiles to spot. After all, the value is in the person. Obvious Stars can be found in the sports, music, film and entertainment industries. However, the highest profile CEOs, salespeople and trainers also achieved their wealth by following their natural path as a Star.

The highest profile Stars are across different industries, including the three Michaels: Michael Jordan, Michael Schumacher and Michael Jackson, every pop star and movie star you could name; outside of the entertainment industry, Stars include Martha Stewart, Oprah Winfrey, Bill Clinton and Anthony Robbins.

The Supporter

The Supporter is outgoing, loyal, reliable and a fantastic networker.

With a blaze frequency, their value is in the heat of the moment – the relationships they create and the wealth of energy, enthusiasm and time they can offer. By linking this resource to a wealth creator, Supporters can create much greater wealth than they could on their own.

Supporter Role Models

Successful Supporters can be found around every very successful wealth creator, whether that profile is a Creator, Star, Mechanic or Deal Maker. However, many Supporters have found success without aligning solely with one wealth Creator. As a result, there are many CEOs of well known, listed companies who are Supporters. You can also find Supporters successfully running businesses in support industries such as PR, recruitment and marketing. High profile supporters include Steve Ballmer, Steve Case, Rudy Giuliani, Jack Welch and Michael Eisner.

The Deal Maker

Successful Deal Makers tend to catch the imagination of the business world, with their sweeping gestures that make millions in a moment. Of all the profiles, the Deal Maker relies most on the relationships around them, as their wealth is created by the connections they make. With a sensory dynamic, Deal Makers are reactive, acting on the right opportunities as they happen.

Deal Maker Role Models

Deal Makers can be found across industries, and the highest profile ones can be seen moving into an industry as it moves past its summer phase, and the bargains can be found, as is happening now with the telco industry. Deal Makers can also be found wherever there exist assets with significant value differentials, such as in property, corporate mergers and acquisitions, and in the entertainment business brokering multi-million dollar brands.

The highest profile Deal Makers include Robert Kravis, Li Ka Shing, Donald Trump, David Geffen and, more notoriously, Don King.

The Trader

As a result of the popularity of online and retail trading, many people see themselves as a Trader. Unfortunately, most are not, which goes to explain why most lose their money. A real Trader is someone who naturally looks for bargains for the fun of it. They love haggling or seeking out the lowest price with the satisfaction that they found it first, and then they are equally good at seeking out the buyer who will pay a higher price. As with the Creator, the Trader can be both introverted and extroverted.

Trader Role Models

Unlike Deal Makers, who make their money without ever owning the assets they are dealing in, Traders will buy and sell the asset, and make their money from the spread. Extrovert Traders will do this where they can influence the price through hard bargaining and can be found in import/export businesses, and the retail industry. Introvert Traders are happy to trade through analysis rather than face-to-face bidding, and include all successful market traders.

The Accumulator

The Accumulator is the safest of the profiles, relying on a system of incremental growth to achieve wealth. The book 'The Millionaire Next Door' is based on the Accumulator profile, as it is one of the most fool-proof to follow. Many wealth seekers adopt the accumulator strategy but either lose patience or get itchy feet and move on. The real, successful Accumulator is patient enough to stick with it, and disciplined enough to keep to their system.

Accumulator Role Models

Accumulators come in two forms. The first accidental Accumulators, are those who made their wealth elsewhere and are now reinvesting their wealth in property, stocks or other vehicles. These are not good role models as they are not the wealth profile of a real Accumulator. The second are those who fit the profile and have made their wealth through their strategy. This includes everyone who has bought and held on to a set of assets over time, whether in company stock, property, land, or any kind of appreciating collectible.

The highest profile Accumulator in the world would have to be Warren Buffet, and there are plenty of books to learn what he did and how he did it.

The Lord

The Lord is the epitome of Stealth Wealth. Rarely seen but rolling in cash, the Lords of the World control everything! They control the land, they control all the natural resources, they control all the man-made structures. They may not own them, but they don't have to. They are too busy counting their money!

Lord Role Models

Successful Lords are not seen, and they are not heard either. With the exception of perhaps the Sultan of Brunei and Saddam Hussein. But Lords are everywhere in every country and in every economy. Lords can be found wherever there is a fixed asset that is generating cash, whether it is a rented property or a leased vehicle, whether it is a gold mine or an oil field.

If you are a Lord, yet have not yet become a successful one, make it your priority to find a mentor who has made it. You will be amazed at how simple the process can be and how fast wealth was created.

The Mechanic

The Mechanic is an enigmatic character who has the ability to control and manage many people without needing to demonstrate any charismatic leadership qualities. His mix of intuitive thinking and systems focus together with a drive to grow and expand leads to the path of expansion through duplication and replication.

Whereas a Star endears, a Mechanic endures. For all successful Mechanics, what they build tends to be built to last.

Mechanic Role Models

Successful Mechanics give Creators a run for their money in the business celebrity stakes. Not only do Mechanics often take over from creators as businesses mature, but they are also capable of starting global, system-based businesses that take on a life of their own as they multiply around the world. Mechanics can be found behind most franchise and multi-chained businesses, and in all manufacturing, distribution, construction and logistics businesses where all creative focus is on the systems rather than the products. The highest profile Mechanics out there include Sam Walton, Ray Kroc, Jeff Bezos and Michael Dell.

Applying Wealth Dynamics

Whilst it is possible to place yourself using the definitions above, taking the Wealth Dynamics profiling test (available from Roger Hamilton www.rogerhamilton.com) will give you a much better result. The test is a self-administered set of questions and the result, which comes from XL, is presented in the form of a diagram (as below for Andy).

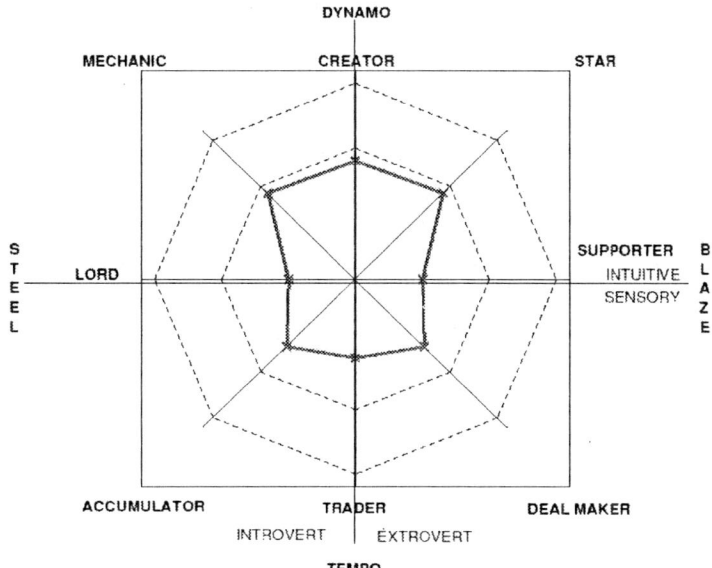

Some results are much more emphatic towards a particular type –
for example Thomas and Penny.

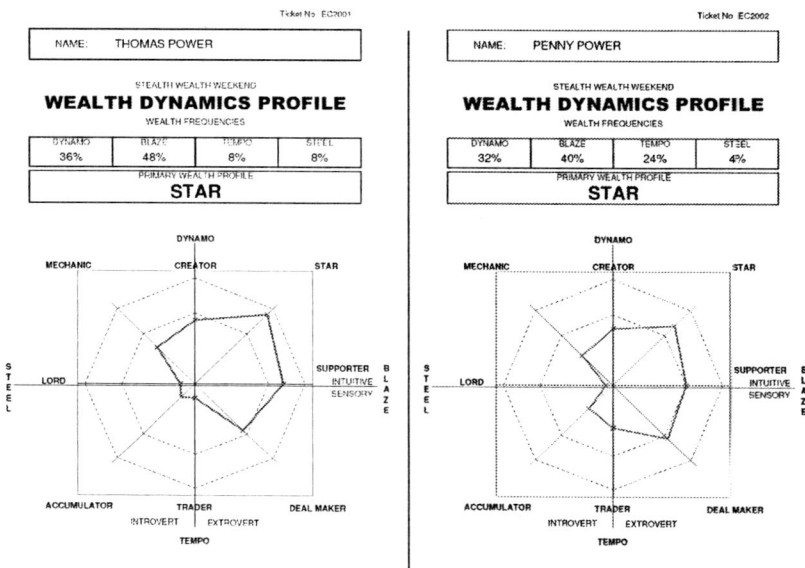

The principal type is supported by some facility in the adjoining
types – so Andy is a Mechanic/Creator/Star whilst Thomas and
Penny are Creator/Star/Supporters. There are many levels of inter-
pretation that can be applied. Those on the left of the square tend
to be Jungian Introverts and those on the right Extroverts.

By drawing a diagonal from Mechanic to Deal Maker, the grid is
divided into two full boxes and four half boxes. They represent
some tendencies towards different stages of the business cycle
from Creator (idea and product) to Mechanic (the system) through
Marketing (Creator/Star/Supporter), coaching, teaching, guiding
(Supporter/Deal Maker), lawyers and sales people (DealMaker/
Trader), accounts and operations (Trader/Accumulator/Lord), engi-
neers (Lord/Mechanic) and Inventors (Mechanic/Creator). As with
all interpretations, they are for guidance and do not define the
person.

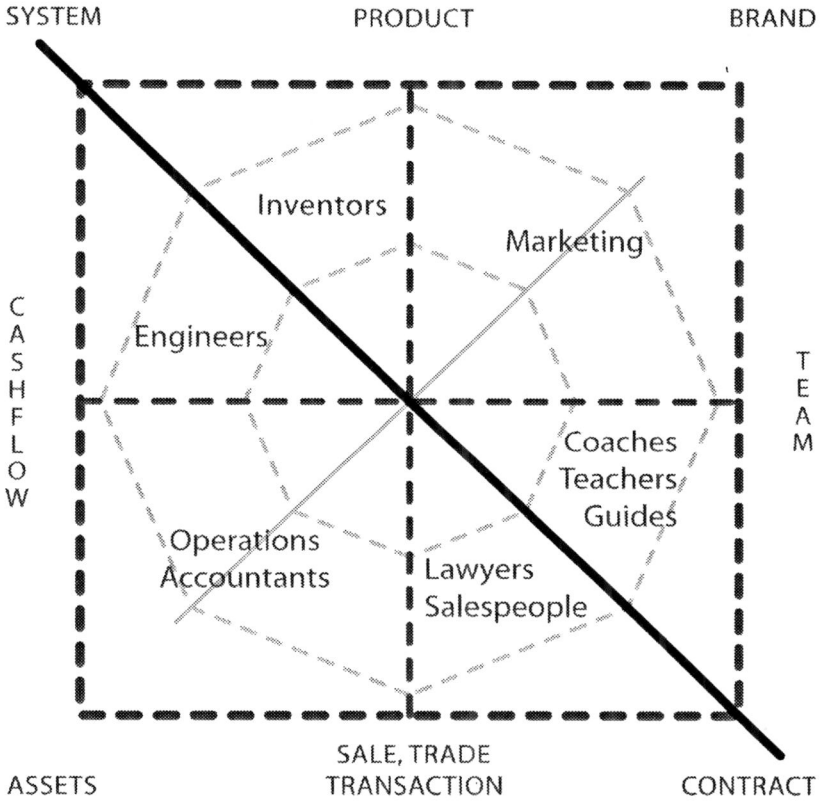

In putting together a team, Wealth Dynamics suggests that you need all eight Wealth Profiles represented. That may not mean having eight people, especially in the early stages of a business, just that with primary and secondary profiles, all bases should be covered.

The emphasis on each profile type will also change as the business progresses through a life cycle, with Creators and Stars needed to generate and develop ideas, Supporters to find the right people, Dealmakers and Traders to make the money, Accumulators and Lords to manage and grow the money and Mechanics to systemise the whole progress.

I n Chapter 10, we introduced you to five types of networker. When you come to building a network, this is the time when you must choose what sort of networker you are and what sort you need to become.

We can't recommend that anyone adopt the **negative** networking position (p 115). The mere fact that the world is changing suggests that it will be network or starve, so if you are here at present, the only way is up.

Being part of a familiar group is something that we all crave, like the **conservative** type. It is comfortable and allows us to make assumptions about the other members of that group. Conservative networking is part of a mix of networking strategies that we all need to follow. Developing deep contact relationships through breakfast groups like BNI and BRE that meet every week, for example, is a very important part of many networkers' strategies. However, we recommend breaching your comfort zone in order to grow and to open up to the possibility of chance or serendipity taking a hand. So, alone, this strategy is not, in our view, a good one.

In many online networks, it is possible for other members to approach you and invite you to be part of their network. Being **reactive** and selective seems like a good strategy. By selecting who is allowed to come into your network, you can exercise control over the ultimate shape of it. In the early stages of networking, it may be a good model to adopt. If, however, you want your networking to really work for you, you need to consider two modifications to this approach. One is saying yes to connections, even where there is no obvious reason to connect. The other is to begin to approach people to connect with who may add new dimensions to your networking. This strategy is still within most people's comfort zone.

Networking **proactively** is what Thomas proposed in *Networking for Life,* and we still commend it as a strategy for the majority of people. It combines the safety of some conservative and reactive networking while allowing for a planned approach to people with whom you might enjoy connecting, who you can help or who may stretch you. Remember that networking is about giving as well as receiving, so be sure of what you have to offer before you adopt this strategy. The rest of this Chapter focuses on approaches that will make this strategy work for you.

Although we commend 'proactive networking' as the best strategy for most people, there are elements of the hyperactive strategy that are useful for all networkers. Some people are hyperactive networkers all of the time (Thomas, for example) but for all of us, it is possible to be 'hyperactive' sometimes. We will try to make the case for quantity leading to quality of connection and talk about connecting randomly. Both approaches need to be considered. So, although most of you will not become full-time hyperactives, a proportion of this strategy is worth including in your mix. After all, you don't know who can help until you've connected, or in which direction random connection could take you.

Many people first come to networking having resigned or been made redundant from a permanent job. Allison McSparron-Edwards, CEO of Consultrix, offers some advice: "Make a long list of all the contacts you have. From that long list, select a small number of trusted people to contact and with them decide whether to go for another job or become self employed. Keep it limited until you know. When you have an understandable proposition, you can go to the rest of your network with it." If you are looking for a job, she suggests, you may be able to select with whom to network. 70% of people get a new job through networking. Bear in mind, however, that Mark Granovetter's research (see below) suggests that weak ties will be more important than strong ones.

McSparron-Edwards concludes: "If you are planning to start a business, get out there and meet people – through events and in one-to-one meetings." Don't forget to connect first at a personal level.

How big a network do I need?

Networking is building relationships that meet the needs of both parties. The more trust that is required to work together, the stronger the tie will need to be. To exchange newsletters or to sell low value services, the level of trust can be lower and the tie weaker. Therefore, it is not all or nothing when discussing network size. You need to consider the ratio of people you need to meet in order to have a network of the required size and strength to achieve your business goals.

There is no optimum network size that works for everyone. As a professional networker, Thomas has a need to grow his network as big as he can make it. Your needs may be more modest, but don't confuse that with trying to meet only 'quality' contacts.

For a start, how will you recognise them? Do they come with a stamp on their forehead marked 'high quality' or 'waste of time'? To listen to some commentators, you might think that this is so. They obsess about approaching only contacts who will be of use. They are the people who speed-read the attendee list at an event, approach, i.e. often try to sell to, the 'key people' there and then leave having decided that the people they didn't meet were not of value to them. Yet until you actually approach and connect with people, you have no evidence on which to make a judgement.

There are lots of people in the world who are of tremendous value to you that you don't yet know – probably more such people than the number you already know. In these circumstances, there will be more value in people you don't know than those you do.

Your network is an asset that needs constant attention and care. We all have business cards that we've collected at meetings and exhibitions, people we've worked with at various companies and suppliers/customers. But are they your network? Some may still be active and valuable but most are probably no longer relevant to where you are now.

That is not to say that they won't be in the future. Christian Mayaud, Venture Capitalist and notable networker, in his blog Sacred Cow Dung, categorises your network into Previously Active (PAN), Currently Active (CAN) and Future Active (FAN). As well as using your CAN for projects and relationships that are happening now, he recommends keeping in touch with your PAN and actively networking to develop your FAN.

Mayaud argues that the CAN for most people will be around 200 to 300 people while "my PAN rose in the normal course of working with different people and companies at different times in my career (currently about 50K). It's my FAN that I don't mind growing online (I never presume to know whether or not I can be helpful to someone someday about something that comes up i.e. I don't feel I have any basis to judge the "quality" of a potential relationship)".

"Technology can help you maintain a high touch relationship with a large number of people. But just how large should that number be?" ask Scott Allen and David Teten, networking commentators and authors of 'The Virtual Handshake', in a Fast Company article in January 2005. Their conclusion is that "The number of your relationships and the average strength of your relationships end up being inversely proportional. The more people you know, the less well you know them. If you want to build stronger relationships, you're going to have to do so with a smaller number of people. You can spend all of your time with your close friends and family (strong ties, low number), or spread yourself across a wide number of people (weak ties, high number). However maintaining both high strength and high number is physically impossible".

Thomas Power contends that your potential income is related to your network size. As it says on his profile, "The winner of the Game is the one with all the names". Those who say that they are looking for fewer, quality contacts, he asserts, are often saying that they can only cope with, say, 200 contacts. They cannot say that only those 200 are high quality and no-one outside that group can be. They say "I've got 200 good contacts – those are the people I do business with and that's enough for me" and that's fine. "However," he continues, "if I say, here's another contact who isn't among your 200 – are you going to say 'I don't want to meet them'. If you've got your group and it never changes, you've got a clique, and cliques decline." The people you do know that want to trade with you, either as a buyer or a seller will contact you anyway because they already know you. "You don't have to make a lot of effort with the people you already know. You have to stay in touch with them".

Some networkers quote a number of 150 as being the largest network that the human brain can control. They often refer to it as Dunbar's number or the Dunbar number. Wikipedia notes that it is a value significant in sociology and anthropology. Proposed by British anthropologist Robin Dunbar, it measures the "cognitive limit to the number of individuals with whom any one person can maintain stable relationships". Dunbar theorises that "this limit is a direct function of relative neocortex size, and that this in turn limits group size...the limit imposed by neocortical processing capacity is simply on the number of individuals with whom a stable inter-personal relationship can be maintained." In a 1993 article, Dunbar used the correlation observed for non-human primates to predict a social group size for humans. Wikipedia continues: "Using a regression equation on data for 36 primate genera, Dunbar predicted a human 'mean group size' of 147.8 (casually represented as 150), a result he considered exploratory due to the large error measure (a 95% confidence interval of 100 to 230)".

So how significant is 150? Professor Dunbar recently commented on the changes that the development of the Internet since the 1993 study may have had upon the number. He points to his 2005 paper titled 'Discrete hierarchical organization of social group sizes' co-written with W.-X. Zhou, D. Sornette and R. A. Hill which he says, "provides the evidence that we (as individuals) seem to sit in the centre of a series of expanding circles of acquaintanceship: as you go outwards, the number of individuals included in each circle increases, but the quality of the relationship (its sense of intimacy) as well as the frequency of contact decline".

Professor Dunbar asserts that the issue here is about both quantity and quality: the two are inextricably mixed. The key point of the 150 number is that this is roughly the limit on the number of individuals that we can know as persons, in a generally intimate kind of way, rather than as individuals. The number of people we know as individuals, where we can put a name to a face, seems to be about 1500-2000, he continues.

The Internet, he contends, provides us with a mechanism that allows us to maintain contact with individuals in situations where 50 years ago they would have dropped slowly off the edge of our radar and it may allow us to maintain a larger (but very low grade) set of relationships.

Reed's Law, first published in 'The Law of the Pack' in Harvard Business Review in 2001 by David P Reed, attempts to create a mathematical model for the number of 'nodes' on a people network and the effect of additional nodes joining it. David Reed sees an exponential growth in possible connections for every node that joins the network, creating huge potential for the existing nodes. The reason for this is that Reed takes into account the number of possible sub-groups of network participants, which is $2^N - N - 1$, where N is the number of participants, whereas Metcalfe's Law (about growth in computer networks) looks at the number of pair connections expressed as $N(N-1)/2$. Thomas' take on this is simple, "David Reed's law suggests that the more transactions you do, the more transactions you will do. You can't have transactions without connections and you can't have connections without attractiveness and you can't be attractive without appeal. So how do you appeal if you are closed? You're saying 'I don't want to meet people.'"

Mark Granovetter acknowledges the differences between weak and strong ties in his 1975 paper on the 'Strength of Weak Ties', suggesting that we need both for successful connections. He notes that "An individual will have a collection of close friends, most of whom are in touch with each other, and a collection of acquaintances, few of whom will know one another. Each of these acquaintances, however, is likely to have close friends in their own right and therefore be enmeshed in a closely-knit clump of social structure. The weak tie between the two densely-knit clumps of close friends becomes not merely a trivial acquaintance tie but rather a crucial bridge between the two densely-knit clumps of close friends. These clumps would not, in fact, be connected to one another at all were it not for the existence of weak ties." The weak ties thus provide a method by which information known to one of these clumps of stronger ties can move between networks and groups providing, for example, early knowledge about available jobs or intelligence about a business requirement.

Using this theory as an approach will lead to the development of a network of both strong and weak ties (or maybe a network where acquaintances are distributed along a continuum between very strong and very weak ties). Strong ties very seldom appear fully formed. They will often begin as a weak tie – maybe someone whose blog drew immediate agreement from you – and the relationship then builds, piece by piece, meeting by meeting. Some ties will remain weak, whilst others will deepen and strengthen. Some ties may never yield any benefit in either direction, but never is a very long time, and the cost of keeping in touch with weak ties, using tools provided by the Social and Business networks, is no longer arduous.

In an article, published in August 2004, in the Toronto Globe and

Mail, headlined 'Never blow off the ones you'll need', James Gray tackles the question of building a manageable network. "If we choose to interact only with those who can benefit us here and now, we're limiting ourselves and possibly our careers. We need to reach out. We need to connect. We need to engage."

The number of people you connect with (your 'reach') is not the same as those you have 'quality' relationships with ('depth'). In a community of 1000 contacts, you will know some of them at a much more intimate level than others. Quality in this case is an index of how important and influential they are to you. It is always a subjective judgement. My quality contact may be unimportant to you.

Learning to Network

Thomas has met 23,000 people in 23 years and as a result he believes that he has become an expert at meeting people online and offline. Meeting and knowing is a matter of experience, and of reading the verbal and visual cues. "With practice you can sense honesty and openness, something to hide, all manner of information to help with connecting."

Practice is the 'secret' that creates champions. They may be born with an innate skill, but it is the practice that trains that skill. Tiger Woods, for example, is known for his obsessive early morning practice routine that involves hitting thousands of golf balls every day, even on days when he will be playing in demanding tournaments. Arnold Palmer once said that "The more I practice, the luckier I get". All of us need, at one level or another, to develop the skills of meeting people and of learning about them quickly.

Don Bradman, the Australian cricketer, was the greatest batsman of his day, and maybe of all time. For those unfamiliar with cricket, the skill of a batsman is to be able to assess each ball bowled at them and hit it according to that assessment. The bat has a flat face which, if hit in the middle, will accelerate the ball in the desired direction. Hit anywhere else, the ball may travel anywhere, putting the batsman at risk of being dismissed. When facing a fast bowler, the amount of time available for the assessment is just over half a second. That is the time it takes for the ball to travel from the bowler's hand to the bat. Bradman would practice his hand-to-eye coordination with a cricket stump and a golf ball, hitting the ball against a wall with the stump hundreds of times at a sitting without missing. If he could master this, with the round section of the stump and the small, bouncy golf ball, he reckoned that he could handle bat on cricket ball. The figures of his career bear this out.

To practice networking is easy: simply get out there and do it. Remember that you are trying to find out as much as possible about the person you are meeting to understand if a relationship (of gives, receives or both) may be possible and worth pursuing. It helps to set a target of meeting and finding out about a number of new people, since our instincts, at least at the start, may be to talk to people we already know.

How did you learn to network? Was it by trial and error, or did you get taught how to do it? For those few who said they were taught, was that as part of a business degree (Bachelor or Masters) at a college? Not many can say yes to that because, as Ivan Misner founder of BNI points out, 88% of a survey of 1400 business people "were never taught networking in college". We suspect the real number is much higher. Dr Misner also notes that "From over 2500 business people, 75% got most of their business through networking" and "82% of all business people belong to some type of network group." We suspect that it will not be long before all business students (and eventually all students?) get a formal Networking 101 module as part of their courses. Networking is an important business and life skill.

Making and Developing Connections

Choosing to be a proactive networker is the first step to building a network. The next is to begin making contact with people at events and online. The process, of course, doesn't end there. A process, call it Network Relationship Management (NRM), has to kick in to make sure you make the most of the opportunities your network brings.

In a Wired Magazine article 'Attention Shoppers!' in 1997, Michael H. Goldhaber talked about attention being the currency of the New Economy. Ecademist Ronald Wopereis talks about Ecademy being 'attention as a product'. Where you give your attention within your network will be where things happen. Attention is like water and nutrients for a houseplant. Provide it, and the connections grow and survive; forget it, and they die. Try to spread your attention across as much of your network as you can, over time, to see it grow.

Approaching events and face-to-face meetings with some idea of what you want to achieve is sensible planning. Executing that plan regardless of what actually happens is not a good idea. Be clear about your objectives, but be flexible in your approach.

Being prepared also means being appropriately dressed for the occasion and having with you business cards and a notebook for making good notes about the people you meet. Those notes will be the basis of your NRM system.

John Kellden of Sign of Knowledge in Sweden came up with a series of networking stages that we all will go through as we progress to win/win/win.

Stage 1 **First blush** — Nervous well-meaning attendees saying and doing all the right things.

Stage 2 **By the book** — Attendees beginning to glimpse the value of the network while still frustrated with it being too fluffy, visionary, English or something else, to serve their needs.

Stage 3 **Tried and true** — Prospective networkers selecting targeted networkers, using an array of business tactics to get prospects and deals.

Stage 4   **Absorb** — Networkers beginning to absorb the connectedness of the network, while still perceiving its prime purpose from a predominantly individual, utilitarian perspective.

Stage 5.   **Clubbing** — Networkers positioning and repositioning themselves so as to get to both bake and eat as much cake as possible.

Stage 6.   **Win/Win/Win** — In which the network becomes the de-facto standard of conducting business built upon friendly relations, with a surrounding ecology of business activities, thriving in a win/win/win mix of collaborative/co-opetitive business models, mental models and business practices.

It would be a mistake and a wasted opportunity, if you were to thrust your business card at each new person you meet whilst gabbling your elevator pitch. Being open to connection is about being interested in the other person and finding out as much as you can about them. There are questions you can ask that will help identify how you can help them. For example "What is your expertise?" "What projects are you working on at present?" and "What contacts are you looking for to help you develop your business?" In an initial meeting, concentrate on the needs of the person in front of you and ask for nothing for yourself.

The person in front of you also brings with them a variety of friends and contacts who by definition are unknown to you on first meeting. So when someone talks about a quality contact, you have to ask yourself if they mean the person themselves or that person's contacts, because neither judgment is one that you can make that quickly. "Like a tree", notes Roger Hamilton of XL Results Foundation, "fruit tends to grow on the outermost twigs" which may be 2 or 3 degrees removed from the person in front of you.

There is much talk about 'elevator pitches' in conjunction with networking. We accept that they have their place. However, whilst it is great to be able to tell someone what you do in 60 seconds or less, it is sometimes more appropriate to just let the conversation flow.

If you choose to approach meetings with no agenda, it is possible to set out in conversation with people even if there is no obvious connection with what you do or what you want. There are no wasted conversations if you are open to the opportunities that, like radio waves, are in the air whenever you meet a new or familiar contact and really allow the conversation to flow.

Be open to the power of coincidence, too. Penny and Thomas have built Ecademy around a number of influences, not least of which is *The Celestine Prophecy* by James Redfield. One of the premises of the book is that coincidences always happen for a reason, that they should never be ignored and always explored. Even if *The Celestine Prophecy* is too new age and spiritual for you, coincidences and synchronicities provide forks in the path of conversation. Sometimes taking 'The Road less Travelled' as Robert Frost wrote, takes you into entirely new and fertile territory. To quote the final lines from Frost's poem (and the basis of M. Scott Peck's famous self-help book):

> *Two roads diverged in a wood*
> *And I took the one less travelled by*
> *And that has made all the difference.*

Conversation should not be a motorway, heading from A to B in the straightest and quickest way. Some should be like English country lanes, green and winding. Set off along one of these lanes and you can enjoy the journey in an unhurried way – after all as Robert Louis Stevenson said: "It is better to travel hopefully than to arrive."

Richard White, Ecademist and expert on Soft Selling, suggests that we use stories to engage with people when networking. Stories are part of our heritage, and can speak to us at a very deep level. At NRG lunches, guests are asked, as part of their introduction, to reveal something about themselves that the other guests won't know. These, often very personal, snippets are frequently the key to remembering people we've met.

Networking is about people first and business later.

Whilst face-to-face communication is familiar to most of us, online communication is still something new and unfamiliar to the majority of business people. We are approaching people who will have little evidence, other than our written words, on which to assess us and our approach to them.

Some people have a formulaic approach to connecting. On Ecademy, this may begin 'thank you for looking at my profile...' These approaches can be counter-productive unless there is evidence that the sender has made some effort to personalise their communications. Find out about the person first – profile, blogs, their network (especially shared connections), Google them – and put something relevant to their interests or background into this message. A shared interest or word from their 50 words will make all the difference.

Making approaches to people with a view to connecting always involves the risk of rejection. Scott Allen has his own rules for making an approach. "In order for me to refer you to people, and you to refer people to me, we have to know something about each other – more than just what's in our profiles. If we don't know any more about each other than is in our profiles, we're not really helping – in fact, we're just in the way of the connection."

"If you want me to help you," Scott continues, "you have to let me know how I can help. What are you looking for? If you want to help me, you have to know what I'm looking for. We have to develop some rapport, some knowledge of each other's professional skills and reputation, etc. A referral reflects on me, and I'm not going to make a referral until I'm reasonably certain it's not going to reflect on me badly. I wouldn't ask it of you, either. Until you know me and know my qualifications, I won't ask you to refer me."

In January, 2006, Christian Mayaud began a club on Yahoo Groups called LinkedIn Lions. His purpose was to make Linkedin management aware that many members disagreed with their plans to restrict the number of invitations that could be sent by members. In LinkedIn's view you should only connect with people you know. The club is growing rapidly with the rallying cry "We talk to strangers". So do we. It seems difficult to imagine how networking can possibly be successful by concentrating only on strong ties.

Nonetheless, it is important to remember that some people do not welcome your approach, and may say so in unequivocal terms. Dr. Ivan Misner, founder of BNI, comments "With online networking, I think that people feel it's easier to be more direct. The problem is that the response is also more direct and may come across as aggressive or antagonistic. So be careful whom you approach, build a relationship before you ask for someone's business. Online networking gives you breadth in your networking efforts. It allows you to broaden your reach to anywhere in the world. Just don't forget that trust and relationship building are still as important as ever".

With conferencing solutions like Skype and Avecomm, it is possible to telephone, videoconference, share applications and whiteboards for low or no cost worldwide. When these tools are combined with your profile on one of the Social Business Networks like Ecademy, a very productive conversation and relationship can follow.

Networking should be blind to differences in gender, race, religion and age. We connect as human beings not as labels. These days it is possible to be a woman in business and get involved in networking through many routes. It wasn't so easy ten years ago, notes Allison McSparron-Edwards: "When I left a high-level job in the City in the early 90s, I set up as a consultant. Being out there, trying to make contacts and have one-to-one meetings was uncomfortable. People didn't expect a woman to be doing that. There were few women in senior positions in business and many networks were male preserves." There is still a need for care when planning to meet one-to-one but there are now many networking groups where men and women are equally represented and equally valued and, of course, there are many women-only groups.

Networking techniques can be used to build relationships with corporates as well as with other small businesses. It is a matter of attitude and a system. Thomas Power proposes that you first pick your corporate and find between 20 and 100 names. Now put yourself in the position of those people and begin to identify connections that they may find useful. When you have good connections for them, send a short note saying "May I come and see you please, I have connections for you". You are likely to get a meeting with this approach, and when you go to that meeting, be sure to arrive with gifts of connections. Whatever you do, at this stage it is important to concentrate on the corporate executive's needs. Go in to solve THEIR problems, not find uses for YOUR product. Who do they want to meet? What connections will help them to develop THEIR projects? Never ask for anything for yourself – if the gives are properly researched, the benefits will flow back.

Our development may be partly planned but is always subject to chance meetings or opportunities. We don't, for example, generally set out to select our life partners according to a checklist of the ideal man/woman. There is a strong likelihood that you 'just bumped into' your partner and discovered that there was an attractiveness to them which led you both down a new path. In his book *Networking for Life*, Thomas Power comments that a key skill in networking will be to increase your 'bumping-into-ness' – giving serendipity a better chance. In other words, the more people you meet, the more serendipity will happen.

Networking can lead to the most unexpected collaborations, though few will have the far-reaching consequences of the relationships that developed between Carl Jung and Wolfgang Pauli. They met when Pauli sought Jung's help with the aftermath of a breakdown in 1931. Pauli became a regular patient of Jung's and began to contribute thoughts to his theories of Synchronicity. It is thought that the exchanges between the two also helped Pauli to his conclusions on Quantum theory. "Despite the fundamental difference between physics and psychology, in their meeting of the minds Jung and Pauli reconnected the meditative and scientific strands in serious alchemy, as well as the complementarities that emerged from William James's philosophy. They linked ancient questions and modern theories and experiments, the interior search of reflective depth psychology and the outward gaze of scientific inquiry" comments Beverley Zabriskie in an Essay *Jung and Pauli: A Meeting of Rare Minds* in the book *Atom and Archetype – The Pauli/Jung Letters, 1932-1958*. Hidden in the welter of communications across the networks, who can know if such connections are being made even as you read this? If they were alive today, Jung and Pauli would certainly use e-mail to conduct their correspondence.

Through conversation, be it face-to-face, telephone or Skype call, e-mail exchanges, forum or club messages, in fact any medium at all, comes understanding and trust. Trust is not like a switch – either on or off. It is a continuum from no trust at all to total trust. What is total trust? It is different things to different people, but consider the trust between the trapeze artist and their catcher, or between horse and rider when galloping towards a hedge at full pace. In both situations, trust is about life and death. Just as trust is a continuum, so our need for trust is also a continuum, from needing none to life or death trust.

Many articles on networking highlight the difference between networking and selling. One key difference many of them point out is one that is integral to Penny and Thomas's approach in Ecademy. That is the idea of giving unselfishly and asking for nothing in return. The best networkers do seem to be generous with their time and their support. There is no balance sheet of gives and receipts – indeed the giver expects no payback at all. Some instead, ask reviewers to pay it forward rather than back and give service and support to someone else. This principle, demonstrated in the film *Pay It Forward* leads to huge loops of paying forward that will, in time, produce receives for the original giver, but probably from an unexpected source. Now, maybe the effect is simply the result of a pay forward giver being more open to the possibilities and opportunities around. Whatever it is, it works and it is the way many people have chosen to live their lives.

Keeping in touch with your network is important. You can use Newsletters to keep in touch with some of your network. Other parts of it will be part of your day-to-day communication. We need to keep track of who we know and when we contact them. Whether you invest in a form of Relationship Management software, use the Social Networks or make the time to contact people personally, it is a task that must be undertaken. One way to do this is to have a place where contacts can interact with you on a regular basis. We will discuss using blogs for this in the next chapter and clubs in the chapter after that.

It is worth mentioning here a concept developed by networker Michael Pockocky (and documented in Dave Taylor's Intuitive Life blog) which he calls 'The Collaborative Concentric Networking Model'. It fits with our own philosophy of using multiple online and offline networks. Michael suggests that you create profiles that are consistent across all networks and that you have a place, on one of the networks, you can build your Collaborative Concentric Network and point connections to it from wherever the initial connection was made. Use this network to "spend your time in collaboration, discussion, communication so that, over time, you will know every member of you network. If your Collaborative Concentric Network club becomes popular, it may become a chargeable club in time".

In *Networking For Life*, Thomas Power talked about the money being in the links not the nodes, and The Cluetrain Manifesto talks of markets being conversations. Combine the two and it becomes clear that the money is in the conversations and the activity in the links. Conversations are opportunities to explore potential and to express needs, wants and dreams. They are also ideal places to give of yourself or of the service you can offer.

Conversations make networks successful and fulfilling.

15 Developing Content

Content, in the form of blogs (weblogs), articles and the threads in clubs and forums, is an excellent way of getting noticed. The Internet is the global equivalent of Speaker's Corner in London's Hyde Park, where you can hear and present ideas on any topic to an audience that will make its views known, often forcefully. If your content is placed well, at high-volume sites, it will be picked up readily by the search engines plus blog consolidators like Technorati and Google Blogsearch, with a resultant increase in your visibility.

As we have mentioned elsewhere, in August, 2005, Technorati reported that they were tracking 14.2 million blogs and over 1.3 billion links. This, they reported, represented a doubling of blogs from March 2005, in just five months. They noted that "the blogosphere continues to double about every 5.5 months". Growth is now 2 million blogs a month.

The focus of Internet activity is moving from web sites to web content. Whilst a website is probably still important for most businesses, they can also use a variety of other sites, social networks, blogging sites, Flickr and other photography sharing sites, del.icio.us and Digg for sharing bookmarks, to put across their message.

The Internet picks up and amplifies good content in a very similar way to audio feedback. Audio feedback is caused when a microphone picks up speaker noise (maybe just a hum) and it is amplified, fed through the speakers, picked up by the microphone, amplified ... and so on. The bloggers are the microphones, sites like Technorati and Google Blogsearch provide the amplifier by making the feeds from blogs available using RSS (Really Simple Syndication) and other methods. Bloggers then find items of interest from other bloggers and blog them and those blogs also find their way to the consolidators. Frequently, conventional newspapers and magazines pick up the latest net buzz. To make this work, two things must happen – new, original and interesting content must be posted and bloggers have to pick up and blog about other people's content. Make sure you do both and you will be noticed and, whilst there is no guarantee, your content may be boosted by the Web's feedback loop.

Some call this' word of mouse' marketing.

Social and business networks that permit content will have their own rules about what can and cannot be posted. Generally speaking, the larger public forums, like the Ecademy front page, need interesting material, preferably original, or signposts to such material, on a range of subjects that might engage the community. Be careful not to make your blog into advertising copy. Its purpose is to inform, educate or entertain. Your profile with commercial and contact information is accessible one click away and most sites allow a signature to include a few lines of links and information as part of the blog.

Smaller more intimate audiences in the clubs will be looking for content that develops an argument or provides relevant information to the topic that the club discusses. Be sure to check if the club allows or encourages commercial content in postings. If they don't, leave your advertising material outside the club.

Whatever the rules of the site, you are responsible for your content and must ensure that it doesn't break the law.

External blogs are used for a wide range of purposes, from personal journal entries through to corporate public relations. Business blogs vary widely from single, often personal, blogs through to multi-author blogs that provide significant knowledge, information and insight. Blogs are often conversations between the blogger and those who add comments, and also quite frequently between bloggers who use each other's blogs to develop a discussion or an argument. It is this interaction in real-time that makes blogs important in developing, shaping and publishing ideas.

In such a large marketplace, getting noticed will require a number of factors – a good network for word-of-mouth promotion, and good reciprocal links with other key blogs in your sector and, above all, great content that is insightful and authentic. Corporate brochure-speak is not enough. It will not be picked up and spread in the way that genuinely insightful and original content will be. In their May 2005 article, 'Blogs will Change your Business', Business Week commented, " Go ahead and belly ache about blogs. But you cannot afford to close your eyes to them, because they are simply the most explosive outbreak in the information world since the Internet itself. And they are going to shake up just about every business – including yours. It doesn't matter whether you're shipping paper clips, pork bellies, or videos of Britney in a bikini, blogs are a phenomenon that you cannot ignore, postpone, or delegate. Given the changes barrelling down upon us, blogs are not a business elective. They are pre-requisite."

Should blogs accept all comments that come their way? The comments on the blog that works in conjunction with this book, www.afriendineverycity.com, are moderated. This means that comments are queued and only published by agreement of the moderator. In our view, most comments which are relevant to the topic and are not personally abusive or thinly veiled adverts for other blogs or spam, will be published. The objective is to stimulate debate and to refine our thinking and that of the readers. Each blogger needs to consider their approach to comments.

Dave Taylor at Intuitive Life has also given this issue some thought, especially as it relates to business blogs. "I believe it's quite reasonable for the company to constantly ask 'is the addition of this content going to make us a more successful company? Are we going to sell more stuff? Attract more customers? Appeal to investors?' Without these questions, a business blog is a corporate initiative gone horribly awry, and will quickly morph into something that is not in the best interest of the company and a disservice to its employees and shareholders. I have always counselled companies to consider their business blog an interactive magazine that they're publishing and managing for the benefit of their customers, market segment and shareholders. This makes it easy to decide whether someone calling your blogger, or CEO, a jerk is submitting a comment worth retaining.".

Who reads blogs? Other bloggers, of course, but who else? *Computerworld* in August 2005 reported that, according to analyst comScore, "Compared to the average Internet user, visitors to blogs tend to be younger and to belong to a wealthier household." They are also more active on the Internet generally. Our experience is that, as sites that provide RSS consolidation proliferate, many more people are becoming aware of, and part of, the 'Blogosphere'. Blogs can be set up to be freestanding or to be part of your website. When included in a website, they make the whole site more attractive to search engines.

An increasing number of corporates are now using blogs to communicate. In some cases, this is as a defence mechanism to counter blogs that question or attack them, whilst in others, it is part of the overall marketing activity.

Once you could control your message, issue press releases, manage the press, spin any bad publicity until its effects were minimised. Now says Business Week, the cost of publishing has reached practically zero. "Any dolt with a working computer and an Internet connection can become a blog publisher in the 10 minutes it takes to sign up. How does the business change when everyone is a potential publisher? A vast new stretch of the information world opens up. For now, it's a digital hinterland. The laws and norms covering fairness, advertising, and liability? They don't exist, not yet anyway. But one thing is clear: companies over the past few centuries have gotten used to shaping their message. Now they are losing control of it."

To counteract this, companies like General Motors are, says *Business Week*, showing their "surprisingly nimble touch with blogs". GM uses them on occasion to steer past its own PR department. Business Week reports that GM Vice-Chairman Bob Lutz has received positive feedback as a result of launching his own Blog 'FastLane'. Lutz received many suggestions and complaints, many of which he posted on his blog with a balanced response. However, GM's strategy is not just based on Lutz. They are also using external bloggers to carry content that could not come directly from the company. "In April the company yanked $10 million in advertising from the Los Angeles Times and demanded that the Times make retractions. Journalists asked GM for specific complaints, and the car company held off. It said it wanted to work quietly with the Times and not battle it out in the press". Instead, Business Week alleges, "GM directed journalists to a blog, AutomoBear.com, that detailed GM's beef. (It had to do with a comparison between two cars, which GM thought was unfair.) Both GM and Miro Pacic, the blogger at AutomoBear, say that GM provided Pacic with information but that no money passed hands".

Business Week's reaction to this is worth considering here: "If GM doesn't pay for positive coverage in blogs, just consider the possibilities in this new footloose media world. There's little to stop companies from quietly buying bloggers' support, or even starting unbranded blogs of their own to promote their products or to tar the competition. This raises all kinds of questions about the ever-shrinking wall between advertising and editorial".

More CEOs are writing blogs and, inevitably, some of those are being ghostwritten for them. In reply to an article by Dave Taylor on his Intuitive Life blog, about whether they are a good thing, Dudu

Mimran responded "I am a CEO blogging for the last 6 months and I can express my opinion about how it contributes to us as an early stage company. Blogging created for me a channel to test new concepts and get immediate responses. Also it works as a great connector for meeting new interesting people. And the most important it gives people the feeling that our company is 'accessible' in a level unparalleled by other mediums". As far as 'fake' CEO blogs were concerned, Nik Kalyani saw this as nothing new. "This is just the good ol' bylined story from print in its digital incarnation." It is, he notes, a lot easier for the PR Agency to place the piece. He does caution: "It does require the CEO or other alleged writer to be more diligent and find out what they have written in case the inquisitive reporter at the afternoon press conference asks for a comment about this morning's post. I can see that back-firing on the company".

Good practice for a Corporate Blog is the topic of an article on the web site of Brook Group (www.brookgroup.com). They note that corporate blogging is a growing trend and offer seven tips to make the blog successful which we paraphrase here:

- **Fine Print** — Blogging can lead to legal issues. Companies should have real concerns about liability, exclusions and limitations, and indemnity.

- **Know What You're Doing** — Senior management should be educated by the corporate communications and legal departments about what blogs are and how they might affect business.

- **Create Blogging Policies** — A company should have a list of policies regarding blogging to ensure that trade secrets are kept secret and personal lives do not become public. Policies may include keeping financial information from being posted, as well as severe consequences for anyone using the blog for negative publicity.

- **Avoid the Marketing Blog** — Making your blog into a blatant marketing campaign is a bad idea. Customers are looking for real answers and honest opinions. They will pick up on insincerity instantly.

- **Keep It Fresh** — Blogs are usually judged by their amount of new content. Easy to add on to, they are designed to be updated constantly. To keep your readers coming back, make your content relevant and timely.

- **Reinforce the Company's Core Values** — Use your blog to reflect your company's inner soul: its mission, goals and direction. It should be consistent with the impression the company wants to make.

- **Encourage Employees to Use It** — Create an atmosphere where they are comfortable asserting their opinions and concerns.

The seven tips in full are at http://www.brookgroup.com/Resources/Web-Marketing/7tips.html.

Blogs are not just about written words. Digital photography, especially phone cameras, has created the need for photo publishing that is being provided by hosting sites like Flickr.com. Once photos are posted on Flickr, they can be made available publicly on the Flickr site, included in other sites by using RSS or included in written blogs. Photo blogging, telling the story of day-to-day life in pictures, is also beginning to grow. The development of the MP3 player for personal listening, especially the Apple iPod, has created a new form of blogging using audio called the podcast. Podcasts are personal radio programmes which may include interviews, commentaries, debates and, of course, music, which are distributed through Web resources like iTunes. The BBC has begun to make some of its programs available in MP3 format to allow listening on an iPod.

With the release in late 2005, of the Apple iPod Video, and new mobile telephone handsets that also handle video, the potential for videocasting (Vodcasting) will grow. With the wide range of video equipment now available, Citizen Television programmes which can be played on the web or on personal video devices now seem set to grow. Pay-per-view programming is also likely to grow, and may pose a threat to the major television services by fragmenting the market, already fragmented by satellite and cable services, even further.

Whether you choose to or not, your name and its associated content is being indexed widely on the Internet. Used well, this distribution of your reputation can be a huge positive force for you and your business. Content that is detrimental to your reputation will also be indexed against your name, so it is a good idea to be aware of this when attempted post something that could downgrade others' views of you.

Blog aggregation into sites like Technorati and Google Blogsearch is important, and getting content there will begin the virtuous feedback loop discussed earlier. Getting your name and keywords on Google and other major Search Engines is, if anything, more important, as most people now use Google as their primary research tool. Blogs get good prominence in Google.

Ecademy is also good for your visibility. Blogs, profiles, marketplace listings and public clubs are all indexed by Google regularly. As Julian Bond, CTO of Ecademy notes, it is a matter of focussing on the right formula, "We're currently telling Google that new listings have appeared and they're getting into the Google Blogsearch in less than an hour. I think they get into the main Google search quicker but I'm not sure how quickly. I'm now working on automatically uploading them to Google Base".

To get the most from this, Julian advises, you need to pay special attention to a number of areas:

- The title should be self explanatory and attract readers to look further.

- The first 250 characters of the listing will be the abstract that Google will show under the title. Short descriptive sentences that quickly convey the listing, work best.

- Google Base lets you use keywords and tags as pivots when searching. So you can go from Ecademy to Ecademy+Jobs to Jobs. So think carefully about which tags to use. It's actually an advantage to use common tags rather than trying to think up new ones.

- Add an image. Google will display this next to the listing. Ideally use an image about the listing but at least put in a logo.

- The first two points apply to blog postings as well.

Remember also that reputation is important here. Don't post blogs simply for Google ratings. Your blogging should always add value to the reader, as should your keywords. Avoid the temptation to use keywords that you think the reader should be using and make sure that you are using keywords that they will actually type into the search box. Marketing through Google will grow and change as the Internet changes, but putting the basics in place now will be a sensible investment and good for your business.

I t is important to be part of as many clubs as you can handle, because much of the activity in networking happens there. Ecademy has almost 2,000 clubs – some active, some not – and a number of other networks including Ryze and openBC have clubs for like-minded (and sometimes unlike-minded) people who have an interest in an area or topic.

Some clubs focus on a geographical area and have mostly face-to-face meetings. BNI, BRE and NRG are examples of the meetings-based club. Others are purely online and many now offer the best of face-to-face and online networking in one club.

Treat a new club or bulletin board as if you were joining a dinner party. Introduce yourself and give some inkling as to why you are interested in that club and its members. Then consider the club to be a conversation between friends.

Involve yourself in the ongoing conversation which is represented by existing threads. Use connections you make doing this to deepen your knowledge of individual club members by debate on a thread or in personal messaging. Add some topics of your own to keep the conversation going, and keep them alive by coming back and commenting. On your thread, you are the host and should not make the mistake of starting a debate and then not taking part in it as it develops.

Start clubs yourself as soon as you are ready to. It helps to know who you are and what you stand for, because it will be soon apparent if you don't. And being a club leader gives you a platform to get known and respected, or to get known and disrespected. You choose your own fate.

Michael Pockocky in his Collaborative Concentric Network model (see chapter 14) suggests that you start a club where you can discuss collaboration and ideas with the network.

As your clubbing develops, you are ready to consider the next stage – the YOU club.

Do you have the basis for creating a club based around your product, service or knowledge? That club may have value associated with membership of it such that you can charge members a subscription from day one, or the value may need to grow from the club itself before members see enough value to begin payment.

Running a small business can be tough. Cash flows, both inward and outbound, can be unpredictable. Planning business growth is made more risky the more unpredictable these flows become. Suppose that there was a way to smooth these flows...

As plumbers and electricians have become more difficult to find, especially in an emergency, services have sprung up from utility providers and insurance companies that use the model of private health care. Each month you pay a relatively small sum and when an emergency arises, a plumber or electrician is dispatched to you. There is a service-level agreement that determines how much you pay for that call out, with the better schemes adding no cost at all. Often there is a fair-use clause in the agreement that allows the service provider a way out if their services are being abused. For most households, the service remains a capability that may be used little or not at all. The service provider is using the income from all of its clients to cover the costs of those who need support.

Businesses can engage various levels of support for IT, accounting,

HR etc using a similar model. The service provider agrees a level of service that is covered by the monthly or annual agreement and the scale of charges that apply. The more comprehensive the monthly or annual payment, the less likely it is that a major unplanned cost will be incurred.

These on-demand services will extend to IT infrastructure – like Grid computing or on demand computing (IBM) where additional processor or disk space will be added as needed to meet peaks in demand as well as high-growth periods. The cost will be calculated on what is used, not on acquisition of expensive hardware. It is a revenue model rather than a capital expenditure one.

The Times reported in May, 2005 on a club for the ex-wives of millionaires called Talaka. Entry to the club is graded up to £25,000 for a year and gives access to networking and advice. Some other examples of what is called fractional ownership include Netjets (www.netjets.com) giving access to executive aircraft, the Whistlejacket Club (www.thewhistlejacketclub.com) for access to yacht cruising in the Caribbean and P1 (www.p1international.com) which gives 'driving time' in luxury and high performance cars.

How might this affect the way you grow a business? You begin by recognising your talent or talents. What is it that you find yourself doing for others – maybe not what you think your business actually is and maybe for now you do it for no cost. Once you know what it is that you offer, you can look at how to commercialise it. If it is product-based, can you supply on a rental basis like on-demand computing? If it is a service, can you make a commercial case for getting a regular income from firms who wish to have access to that service in an emergency or on a priority basis? If what you provide is knowledge or information-based, can you find a group of people or firms will benefit from getting access to your knowledge or information on a regular basis?

Ecademy is a club where the network had to build before charging structures were put in place. Networking was not a well-understood concept in the early years, and there was a need to demonstrate a viable network in operation. More recent networking sites are putting charging in place from inception or in the very early days of operation. The value proposition is now much better established.

The life membership scheme for Ecademy and the BlackStar network that it created, was chargeable from its inception in 2004. The fact that over 200 BlackStar members have chosen to pay a significant fee to become life members is testament to the value proposition that they see there. Life membership continues to be offered to a limited number of people each year, and the cost of entry is expected to rise with the growing value of the network. It is not for everyone. BlackStar has its strong critics who see it as elitist and divisive.

Those who have joined BlackStar have done so for a variety of differing reasons. Some are using the contacts and access to people to grow existing business, some to develop new businesses, some are finding new friends and social relationships. Most are finding the camaraderie and energy of the membership to be a distinct benefit in their daily lives. Recruitment continues year on year. With the joining fee currently £4,000 with increments each year, there appears to be no shortage of prospective members.

Chargeable clubs are unlimited in their scope. They may be modelled on the plumbing example, where your product or service is available in an emergency, or they may become like publishing part works, where subscribers receive knowledge and insight regularly. Some firms may choose to use chargeable clubs to give access to their products or services to early adopters, offering benefits to them in return for feedback into R&D activity. They may also form the basis of fractional work schemes, with both customers and freelance contractors paying to be part of a requirements, matching service using models borrowed from consulting firms and IT service providers.

Some Chargeable clubs will offer quality consulting labour 'on demand'. BlackStar will become a key business model in the future for skilled consultants who cannot sell their time any more for $1000 - $2000 per day.

Chargeable clubs offering good service and value for money will be popular with small businesses who can take subscriptions to enable them to concentrate on the core of their own business development. They may be operated by sole traders or by teams, and they may become substantial businesses in their own right. What will distinguish them is the on-demand approach with a subscription model.

Current networks offer a range of services and possibilities that allow individuals or groups to share information, take action, develop strong connections and to exercise their creativity. Networks are the sum of their members – they enable members and provide them with tools.

If networks fulfil their promise, they will become the 'work bringers' for some and resource finders for others. Creating a balance of work available and work needed is a dream, but not one that is impossible.

As we write, not all online networks are accessible by everyone. The Digital Divide – between those with unfettered access to computer networks and those without – remains a major barrier. It works at macro and micro economic levels. Large parts of the continents of Africa, Asia and South America currently lack the infrastructure to enable networks for their people. For large numbers of people, for example, the more than 840 million people who are living in a state of chronic, persistent hunger, dealing with hunger, disease and lack of shelter will be a prerequisite to dealing with the Digital Divide.

Even in the more affluent areas of those continents, and in Europe and North America, groups of people lack the personal economic or educational resources to be able to use electronic networks. A number of initiatives are developing to create low-cost computers that will give access to the Internet. Many are based around the LINUX operating system. An educational need, though, will replace the technical digital divide. Using networks requires good reading and writing skills, and these cannot be taken for granted in the areas where economic prosperity is absent. Moving towards podcasting and vodcasting may help to overcome the barriers of education.

Much more difficult to overcome are the political barriers faced by people in some nations. Access to the Internet, or to specified parts of it, is illegal in some countries – perhaps because of the free access to news and opinions which some nations do not wish their citizens to see. Information, claim the proponents of the Web, wants to be free. Some nations and religious groups would prefer that it is not. There is much to do in these areas.

In June, 2005, Oxford University launched a 'unique' collaborative research centre putting it "at the forefront of research to find solutions to the most pressing problems facing the world in the 21st century". The James Martin 21st Century School, funded by a multi-million pound endowment by British-born computing pioneer James Martin, will stimulate research on issues such as climate change, an increasingly ageing society, extreme inequalities in wealth across countries and continents, the risk of infectious disease epidemics like AIDS and SARS, and the effects of rapid technological change.

As to what networks might become, there are some business models already apparent, and others may develop. Of those that we can foresee, there are three that look most likely to continue.

Earlier in this book we talked about 'triangles of trust' where a third party provides the trusted links between parties who cannot trust each other directly. Online networks are, like the Guilds of the middle ages, just groups of people who have chosen to join together. Their activity within the network and with other members will create their reputation. As reputation systems become better managed and trusted, networks will be able to provide a trusted intermediary service between people and a trusted infomediary service for information sources. If you want people or information to depend upon, networks will be one of the sources to trust. Guilds evolved into Mutuals, into Building Societies, into Insurance Companies and into Banks. Some Networks will evolve into the Trusted institutions of the future.

Closely related to the intermediary route, is the development of networks into alternative media. The Googlezon video (see Chapter 6) which circulated in 2005 takes an apocalyptic view of the development of Google and Amazon over the next few years until, having acquired all other Internet companies (like eBay, Yahoo etc.), they merge to become Googlezon. The video, set in 2014, begins with the final closure of the New York Times and the death of real news reporting. The future may not develop in such a dark way, but the use of networks to provide news reporting and feature writing – effectively content rich newspapers and magazines – is not only possible but is beginning to happen now. Podcasting and vodcasting may become the Radio and Television of choice for many as more content becomes available 'on demand'. Many of the sources quoted in this book were first brought to our attention through blogs on the Internet and, in many cases, on Ecademy. It is in our power to make the information and reporting on the Internet more balanced and accurate by choosing what we read and how we behave online.

Networking is already entering the classroom and university lecture hall. It is possible to educate people remotely by distance learning (as the Open University in the UK has proved) and to increase the amount of material that is delivered online. Broadband technologies have made it possible to deliver multimedia educational modules on demand, backed up by discussion forums and other tools to link students from across the globe into a single student body. Podcasting and vodcasting will also be critical technologies here. If we can download modules and listen to or view them when or where we like, we can take control of our education and development.

For the freelance worker, the ability to get education and support online and at a time that suits them, will drive the development of networks to deliver all manner of courses and modules.

People who connect in Business Networks find that, as well as being purposeful about business, they socialise with other members and create great friendships independent of geography – hence the title of this book. This social element of the networks will, increasingly, be reflected in the development of social enterprises and social activism. Social Enterprises are businesses set up to produce results for a wider group of stakeholders and causes than is typical in commercial enterprises. Social activism has already created its own networks, sometimes covert, to allow activists to share knowledge and to build common purpose. There is a spectrum of social activism from purely benevolent – for example charitable responses to the Asian Tsunami – to purely malevolent groups who use direct action to deliver fear and violence. Open networks are more likely to host the former but may be subject to entryism by darker forces. It suggests a need for vigilance in the management of such networks.

Ecademy will continue to provide a place where members can build a long-lasting friendship, have access to knowledge and resources and can meet each other online and face to face.

Development for Individuals

The constant growth of potential connections across the networks that exist now and will exist in the future seems inevitable. The generations that are coming into business today – and will run it in the not too distant future – are already comfortable with technology. They text, IM and e-mail each other and take active part in online forums and chat rooms from an early age. Their demands on technology will drive the development of better interfaces and more certainty in building trusted relationships online.

The growth of knowledge provided by these people over years of operation, coupled with excellence in matching engines, will create a collective knowledge base which is easily accessed and used. As our ability to create thinking computers improves, we will have something that looks and behaves like a collective brain.

Having the capability and using it are, of course, different issues. To make the most of this collective brain, we may have to undertake a significant shift in our thinking.

A number of writers and thinkers have considered the connectedness of humanity:

- Buddhist philosophy suggests that we are all outcrops of the collective consciousness

- Carl Jung suggested that we share a collective unconscious in which many of our cultural norms are stored to be used as we develop

- Pierre Teilhard de Chardin whose book 'The Phenomenon of Man' suggests that the Noosphere (again a type of group mind which de Chardin sees as encircling the earth like the atmosphere) can raise our thinking to a whole new level of common understanding.

- Dan Pink whose 2005 book 'A Whole New Mind' suggested a move from the information age to the Conceptual Age and with it a change in human thinking from mostly left brain and orderly to right brain and creative.

Ken Wilber in his book 'A Theory of Everything' believes that we are on the verge of a shift from the green meme of Spiral Dynamics, which is pluralistic, allowing for many theories and concepts but seeing the difference between them, to the yellow meme, which is holistic, that is still allowing for many things and concepts but seeing the link between them. Networks and people, working together, can make the "huge leap" from one level to the next and continue the development of people up the spiral.

Networking can, and we believe will, deliver more emotionally intelligent and emotionally wealthy individuals who work with each other to develop win-win solutions rather than trying to cut each other out of deals. We will see a move to a more empathic generation.

Along with Wilber and his integralist approach are others who are trying to help this leap take place. Andrew Cohen, founder of the magazine *What is Enlightenment* is working with a number of committed people to bring about Evolutionary Enlightenment. Cohen's goal is to work towards a higher consciousness and to create a blueprint for a new culture beyond ego. "We have the potential to bring into this world a New Being. It is a new organism, a new consciousness made up of independent, autonomous individuals."

Another Ecademist, Alex Goodall, is working on a plan, The Life Learning Project, to deliver education and support for the potential leaders of the world, so that they can operate at a higher point on the spiral than most of their citizens. The idea is to spread a holistic view of human relations around the world and "help provide our future leaders with the vision, wisdom and skills they will need to ensure the survival and evolution of humanity into the 22nd Century".

Once we have enough individuals connected through networks and the networks themselves working together, maybe we can help the move towards some ideals. The tipping point may come when we have sufficient members from a diversity of backgrounds. Networks are, with some limitations, transcendent of all barriers. They can connect people across nations, religions, race, gender and political affiliation.

Growth of network membership as a whole is inevitable and growing faster. At a time when the memberships have grown sufficiently, we can begin to persuade the world's politicians that humanity is our common core and propose peace not war, understanding not argument, and conversations not conflict. Networks can become a force for the greater good. As Winston

Churchill once said "Jaw-jaw is better than War-War". It is a long and probably arduous path, but if we can grow the pressure for change person by person, conversation by conversation then maybe we can leave a legacy for generations to come.

Providing a significant number of people with a better life and with friends from around the world will be good, too – but can we change the world?

We'd like to think that we could. Are you willing to be part of that?

Any big goal, as this undoubtedly is, can only be achieved step by step. The step for this stage of the 21st Century is to connect with people and, especially, to connect across barriers. If we can get the world talking, we can begin to talk about the things that matter to us and attempt an understanding of each other's values, our different Emotional Wealth. That's why we strongly believe that we need to have at least one friend in every city across the world. If we do, maybe the generations to come will start from this foundation of better communication and build further.

A Friend in Every City, which remains the aim of Ecademy, is about leaving a legacy for our children and our children's children. Ecademy is aiming to have 100 PowerNetworkers in a 100,000 towns worldwide by 2050 – that's 10 million PowerNetworkers. "That's a £1 billion business" Thomas notes "And a £1 billion business right now seems a long way off. Is it achievable? Yes it is! Are the people there to join it? Yes there are!" Most importantly, 10 million networkers represent a powerful movement with the potential to make a real difference in the world. As Mahatma Gandhi once exhorted, we need "to be the change we want to see in the world.".

The debate begins here. There have already been developments to the topics in this book that we could not include. We will document these at the blog (www.afriendineverycity.com) that accompanies this book. Please join us there and put your point of view.

Appendix 1

Edited Extract from Networking for Life by Thomas Power

Chapter 10 - The Ten Steps of Networking

Many people have asked me to encapsulate my approach to power networking, and this set of ten steps is the result. These aren't commandments, nor are they laws. They are simply the ten sorts of things you need to do to become a successful networker, based on my personal experience, my observations of the growth of Ecademy, and the lessons I have learned from my contacts. Put these ten steps to work for yourself, and networking will rapidly become second nature to you. These steps are simply habits of awareness. See yourself as someone who networks, and that's who you'll be.

Step One: Collect People

Be obsessed with collecting email addresses. In January 1999 I had 300 people in my Outlook contacts file. By January 2003 I had exactly 11,980. This means I had been collecting people at the rate of 250 per month for 49 months. Believe me, this is seriously hard work. It takes around eighty to one hundred hours of personal networking online and offline each week. I am not talking about buying a spam list for $199.00. I'm talking about real graft walking the world's pavements. In this time I have spoken in thirty countries, written four books and had 4,000 face-to-face meetings. There's no escape from the arithmetic of networking. Put the time in, and build your networked world, person by person.

Step Two: Respect Geography

I spent four years working for Urban Science in Detroit, where I learned to appreciate that most people spend 80% of their income within two miles of their front door. This means that you should focus on your local network before your international network. It's easy to use e-mail contacts to spread yourself widely, but true networking is about face-to-face meetings. Get a handle on networking in your neighbourhood, and you'll learn the skills and habits for networking on a wider scale. You'll also meet more potential value more quickly. Five thousand of my personal contacts are in London. My partner Penny knows more than three hundred families in Farnham, our home town. My brother-in-law knows 5,000 people in the French city of Toulon, where he owns a hotel. You can also use geography to deepen your network in pockets as you travel. If you travel as part of your job, research the area you're visiting before you go. Find out where people meet. Look through Ecademists who live or work in the same area, and see if you can offer them anything while you're in their neighbourhood. Eat with them, and get the sense of the places they live in. Your travels will become much more exciting as you see and learn much more than the isolated traveller sees.

Step Three: Start a Club

Think carefully about your topic, and then create a club for interested people. Your topic need not be business. We chose ebusiness at Ecademy, but it could have easily been Marketing, or Football, or Gliding, or Embroidery. If you need help to decide on what club you should form, try using Marcus Buckingham and Donald O. Clifton's book Now, Discover Your Strengths (Free Press, 2002). This book concentrates on finding your strengths and playing to them. This can be a good way of finding out where your real passions lie, and also point you in the right direction for leading your club. But you need to be first in the field. You also need to invest time in your club, recruiting members, creating interesting material, and organising events. Be first and go fast. Remember: The winner of the game is the one with all the names.

Step Four: Relax

Networking is a uniquely human activity. We're programmed to get along with each other, as well as to compete. But we hear more about competition than cooperation. Our informal education in business, and the messages we absorb from the entertainment media, focus on conflict, and strategy, and quick-wittedness. Competing is all about adrenalin. Networking isn't about sudden wins, but protracted relationships. We look for the strengths in our contacts, rather than looking for weaknesses in "opponents". Networking is a social activity, so successful networkers make sure that their encounters are comfortable, non-threatening, and conducive to sharing. In many societies, alcohol is a social lubricant. It relaxes the natural inhibition, fear and apprehension that go along with meeting new people. I'm not promoting alcoholism, nor am I against those who don't drink. Alcohol is a depressant, and we have to use it wisely. But alcohol is one reason why effective networking often takes place in bars, over lunch or at parties. Don't be afraid to use any technique for putting yourself and other people at ease. Your choice of venue can have a huge influence on an encounter, as can your dress code. Ecademists can be found networking in coffee shops, country pubs, motorway service stations and back gardens, as well as the more traditional venues in offices, hotels and clubs such as the Institute of Directors in London. Pick the level of formality that suits you, and you'll remove many of the unconscious barriers to successful networking.

Step Five: Go for Volume

You cannot build a "quality network". There is no such thing. Think about it. If you could have a "quality network", then you'd be saying that some people are "quality", and others aren't. But that's not the way it works. Welcome everyone into your network: big or small, rich or poor, gay or straight, white or black. These things do not matter. These things are called prejudice. Prejudice stops you thinking, stops you listening, and ultimately stops you succeeding. The only thing that matters in your network is volume. Make sure you meet twenty people per week, eighty people per month and 1,000 people per year. Commit these targets to memory. You need volume in your network because the money's in the links not the nodes. In the world of networking, you do not know what you are seeking until you find it. You may be seeking a job, or knowledge, or some kind of transaction. Chances are, you will think you're seeking one goal but your network will produce other goals that are actually closer to your needs. But without volume in your network, there won't be enough links to produce the outcome you need.

Step Six: Listen for Link Words

When I am in meeting with someone, I ask 'open' questions. Open questions often start with one of the six great 'w' questions: who, what, why, when, where and how. ('How' is an honorary 'w' question, by long-standing tradition!) An open question doesn't contain any prompting for a particular answer. Then I shut up, and listen, and make copious notes. My notes are so copious that I consume a Moleskine notebook each and every month (see www. moleskine.com). Moleskine notebooks were used by the likes of Van Gogh and Hemingway – so they'll do for me. Try one for a month. Notebooks also make great journals, providing sanctuary from the stresses of daily life. You might be using a PDA (Personal Digital Assistant) to organise your life, but that's unlikely to be the right tool for capturing your most personal thoughts. Use old technology notebooks to write down your worries, your goals and your dreams. Tell your notebook about your loneliness and your concerns. Challenge your negative thoughts as they occur. I'm an advocate of online tools: but there's something about the process of writing with a pen on paper, in your own private notebook, which connects directly with the head and heart. It's vital that you listen for link words and write them down. You should collect fifty link words at each meeting. Do not leave the meeting until you have gathered those fifty link words. The meeting's not over until you have your fifty. You must also review your notebooks at the end of each day so that your mind can ponder link words overnight. Great links will emerge in your mind. Never forget: the money's in the links not the nodes. So you must collect people, go for volume, and gather link words. This is the science of networks. Be sure to re-read your notebooks at the end of every month, and at times when you're looking for a fresh thought or angle. Never throw your books away. They'll be useful when you write your memoirs. As you travel through the world, meeting people and listening hard to what they have to say, and helping to connect them with each other, you are weaving a fascinating story of life in our massively connected world. Those notes are to be treasured. They are as valuable as your family photographs. They are recording your life, your growth, your development and your richness. They become a testament to the good you have done in the world.

Step Seven: Create Matches

Once you have had time to ponder the links words you have collected, you must make connections. Be a matchmaker. Use the Ecademy member directory to put people together. Don't think about "what's in it for me". Think about what might be in it for them. Then simply make the connection and move on. The more connections you make, the larger your network becomes. Not every connection generates financial wealth for you. In fact, only some one in fifty connections generates direct wealth for you. But the remaining forty-nine connections generate reputation, knowledge, kindness, politeness, peace of mind and many free lunches. This is wealth also. Happiness is wealth. Friends are wealth. Networks are wealth. Do not be blinded by your need for financial transactions. They're a small part of the picture. The billionaire oil magnate and philanthropist John D. Rockefeller, Jr. said: "The poorest man I know is the man who has nothing but money."

Step Eight: Disturb Your Comfort Zone

That's right: do something that disrupts your normal, comfortable pattern. None of us likes doing this. But we're all better off for doing it. It means reading books you don't like, as well as the ones you do. It means reading magazines designed for a different target group. It means going to events and networking sessions you consider irrelevant. It means putting yourself in the wrong places, at the wrong times, with the wrong people. That is the value of Step Eight. The point is to release your subconscious mind, to open it to novel materials that may reveal new links. You are already creating volume, listening for link words and letting your conscious and unconscious mind process those links. By disturbing your comfort zone, you enlarge your mind's processing capacity. It's like magnifying the volume of your network, or – more closely – having more than one brain on the job. And sometimes you will discover that the tastes you thought you always had weren't quite right. Or that some group you dismissed as irrelevant has something sensible to say after all. Many people ignore Step Eight. But it is a powerful way of accelerating and deepening your networking activity. Disturbing your comfort zone on a regular basis is a sure-fire way to keep learning and growing. Surprise yourself!

Step Nine: Read

Yes, not only am I an evangelist of the online economy who writes with a pen in notebooks, I'm also a modern communicator who believes in the ancient technology of reading. Reading is the key skill of the new economy. It's not 'computer literacy', which just means the ability to use an interface. Being able to use technology will help you find the information you need, but you need to apply your brain before that information is any use in the real world.

No time to read? Groucho Marx said: "I find television very educational. Every time someone switches it on, I go into another room and read a good book."

I read a book each and every week. Make sure you read regularly, even if you simply re-read your notebooks (see Step Six). Read offline, read online, read on the loo, read on the train, read on the plane, read in bed. Read, read, and read. Did I mention that you should read?

Step Ten: Manage your Reputation

Take care of your reputation. Guard it both online and off. Your reputation isn't the same as your character, but it is your character's proxy. In other words, in the social world, your reputation is you. And your reputation will outlive you. If you make an error that affects your reputation online or off, apologise and make amends immediately. Keep your reputation in good repair. Think of it as a dimension of your health. Think of it as your place in history. A simple and direct way of building your reputation is to gather written testimonials. It surprises me how few people ask for positive feedback in this way. Yet we are all interested in objective feedback from people on how someone has performed, or how she has added value. When something goes right, ask the people involved if they'll write a few words saying so. More often than not, they'll be happy to oblige. Putting their feedback in writing is an excellent means of sealing a transaction or a relationship, and costs nothing. People like to have their opinions known. Never forget that your face is your brand. Spread that face around the place and keep it looking good. Exercise, eat and sleep well. You are your most valuable business tool, so invest in your upkeep and development.

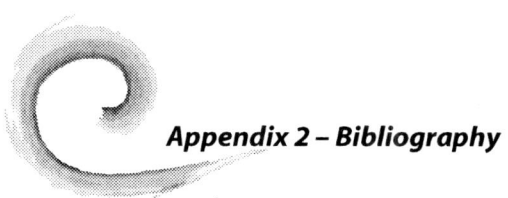

Appendix 2 – Bibliography

Blogs and Websites referred to in this book

This is a list of references which is as complete as we can make it. The references here, with additional links added after publication, will appear on the blog that accompanies the book at www. afriendineverycity.com.

Chapter 1

Ten Laws of the Modern World by Rich Karlgaard, Forbes.com April 2005, (Gilder's Law): http://www.forbes.com/business/free_forbes/2005/0509/033.html

Zopa: http://www.zopa.com/ZopaWeb/

The Demographic Shape of Things to Come by Adair Turner, Global Agenda Magazine: http://www.globalagendamagazine.com/2004/adairturner.asp

Association of Consulting Actuaries: http://www.aca.org.uk/index.asp

The UK Pensions Commission Second Report
http://www.pensionscommission.org.uk/publications/2005/annrep/annrep-index.asp

Small Business Trends blog by Anita Campbell:
http://www.smallbiztrends.com/

The Coase Theorem: http://en.wikipedia.org/wiki/Coase_theorem

The Silver Fox Network: http://www.silverfoxvp.com/index.htm

Wisdom Bank: http://www.wisdombank.co.uk/

Jim Tuffin of Biztime: http://www.ecademy.com/account.php?id=44055

Chapter 2

Revisiting Emotional Wealth Building 101 Tobin Smith:
http://www.money-talk.org/viewtopic.php?p=2159&highlight=

Chapter 3

Content is not King, Andrew Odlyzko, First Monday:
http://www.firstmonday.org/issues/issue6_2/odlyzko/

The Long Tail Chris Anderson, Wired magazine:
http://www.wired.com/wired/archive/12.10/tail.html

Coase's Ideas Flourish in the Internet Economy article by Bob Tedeschi, New York Times, in 2000: http://www.law.uchicago.edu/news/coase.html

The Pro-Am revolution by Charles Leadbeater and Paul Miller (Demos 2004):
www.demos.co.uk/proamrevolutionfinal_pdf_media_public.aspx

Chapter 4

Five reasons social networking doesn't work by Molly Wood CNET, June, 2005:
http://www.cnet.com/4520-6033_1-6240543-1.html

Friendster, Love and Money Gary Rivlin, New York Times January, 2005:
http://www.nytimes.com/2005/01/24/technology/24network.html?ex=1264309 200&en=06a02bfb20b2b6c0&ei=5090&partner=rssuserland

Why MySpace is the Hot Place by Steve Rosenbush, Business Week, May 2005:
http://www.businessweek.com/magazine/content/05_24/b3937077_mz063.htm

Google site 'used by drug gang' BBC News July 2005:
http://news.bbc.co.uk/1/hi/technology/4706489.stm

Bill Thompson's network BBC News:
http://news.bbc.co.uk/1/hi/technology/3505654.stm

MySpace and FaceBook, Om Malik Business 2.0 in May 2005: http://money.cnn.com/magazines/business2/business2_archive/2005/06/01/8263465/index.htm

comScore Media Metrix: http://www.comscore.com/metrix/default.asp

Craig Newmark, *Craig blog*: http://www.cnewmark.com/

Steve Rubel's blog *Micropersuasion*: http://www.micropersuasion.com/

The Virtual Handshake blog, David Teten and Scott Allen:
http://onlinebusinessnetworks.com/blog/

Jim Dickie, *destinationCRM*:
http://www.destinationcrm.com/articles/default.asp?ArticleID=4789

Diane E. Lewis for the Boston Globe in May 2005: http://www.boston.com/business/technology/articles/2005/05/30/job_sites_stress_insider_angle/

Electronic Privacy Information Centre (EPIC): http://www.epic.org/

interview with Reid Hoffman in nPost:
http://npost.com/interview.jsp?intID=INT00079

Chapter 6

Googlezon video by Robin Sloan and Matt Thompson:
http://www.robinsloan.com/epic/

What eBay could learn from Craigslist by Randall Stross, New York Times June 2005:
http://www.nytimes.com/2005/06/05/business/yourmoney/05digi.html?ei=509
0&en=c615dd4899610eca&ex=1275624000&adxnnl=1&partner=rssuserland&e
mc=rss&adxnnlx=1142942798-BSs8dDgdj3DROG4yeLqBkA

Electronic Frontier Foundation: http://www.eff.org/

Cory Doctorow: http://en.wikipedia.org/wiki/Cory_Doctorow

Sysinternals blog by Mark Russinovich:
http://www.sysinternals.com/blog/2005/10/sony-rootkits-and-digital-rights.html

Stowe Boyd, Darwin Magazine:
http://www.darwinmag.com/read/010104/context.html

Chapter 7

Ki work: http://www.ki-work.com/

Ecademy Corporate Services (ECS):
http://www.ecademy.com/node.php?id=56512

Hungry Week: http://www.hungryweek.org/

The Flame Insitute: http://www.theflameinstitute.com/

John Cave and Sam Thiara, Westhaven Logistics:
http://westhavenww.co.uk/home

Business to Business Networking and its Impact on Innovation: Exploring the UK Evidence, Luke Pittaway and Maxine Robertson of Lancaster University Management School:
http://www.lums.lancs.ac.uk/publications/viewpdf/000277/

Working the Net, C. J. Prince, Entrepreneur magazine (July 2005): http://www.
entrepreneur.com/Magazines/Copy_of_MA_SegArticle/0,4453,321901,00.html

Chapter 8

Ebay and Live8 tickets, Wired magazine:
http://wired.com/news/culture/0,1284,67857,00.html?tw=wn_tophead_5

Chapter 9

Measuring the Influence of Bloggers on Corporate Reputation, White Paper from Onalytica December, 2005:
http://www.onalytica.com/MeasuringBloggerInfluence61205.pdf

American Express RED card:
http://www.americanexpress.com/pes/uk/benefits/red/microsite/index.shtml

Nestle – *Our Responsibility*:
http://www.nestle.com/Our_Responsibility/Responsibility.htm

Marks and Spencer Fairtrade: http://www2.marksandspencer.com/thecompany/mediacentre/pressreleases/2006/com2006-03-06-00.shtml

Chapter 10

Five Types of Networkers, Bjørn Guldager, Ecademy:
http://www.ecademy.com/node.php?id=58291

Chapter 11

The Johari window: http://www.augsburg.edu/education/edc210/johari.html

Chapter 12

Personality Plus by Malcolm Gladwell, New Yorker magazine September 20th 2004: http://www.gladwell.com/2004/2004_09_20_a_personality.html

The Graves Spiral: http://www.braintechnologies.com/clare_graves.htm

Spiral Dynamics (SD): http://www.spiraldynamicsgroup.com/

The works of Carl Jung (1875 - 1961): http://www.ship.edu/~cgboeree/jung.html

Myers Briggs Type Indicator (MBTI):
http://www.teamtechnology.co.uk/tt/t-articl/mb-simpl.htm

Chapter 13

I Ching (Book of Changes): http://www.iging.com/

Chapter 14

Consultrix: http://www.consultrix.co.uk/index.html

Sacred Cow Dung blog, Christian Mayaud: http://www.sacredcowdung.com/

The Great Debate: Quality or Quantity?, Scott Allen and David Teten, Fast Company January 2005:
http://www.fastcompany.com/resources/networking/teten-allen/010305.html

Co-Evolution Of Neocortex Size, Group Size And Language In Humans, R.I.M Dunbar 1993: http://www.bbsonline.org/documents/a/00/00/05/65/bbs00000565-00/bbs.dunbar.html

Discrete hierarchical organization of social group sizes, W.-X. Zhou, D. Sornette, R. A. Hill and R.I.M Dunbar 2005:
http://www.journals.royalsoc.ac.uk/(rxrcbq453x5dvpqmrdxt3445)/app/home/contribution.asp?referrer=parent&backto=issue,12,14;journal,30,219;linkingpublicationresults,1:102024,1

That Sneaky Exponential—Beyond Metcalfe's Law to the Power of Community Building by David P Reed: http://www.reed.com/Papers/GFN/reedslaw.html

Metcalfe's Law: http://en.wikipedia.org/wiki/Metcalfe's_law

The Strength Of Weak Ties: A Network Theory Revisited by Mark Granovetter: http://www.si.umich.edu/~rfrost/courses/SI110/readings/In_Out_and_Beyond/Granovetter.pdf

Never blow off the ones you'll need, James Gray Toronto Globe and Mail: http://preview.hrpao.org/HRPAO/KnowledgeCentre/newscluster3/Never+Blow+Off+the+Ones+You%E2%80%99ll+Need.htm?print=true

Ivan Misner founder of BNI: http://www.bni.com/default.aspx?DN=224,1,Documents

Attention Shoppers! by Michael H. Goldhaber, Wired Magazine 1997: http://www.wired.com/wired/archive/12.07/shoppers.html

LinkedIn Lions: http://finance.groups.yahoo.com/group/linkedinlions/

Essay *Jung and Pauli: A Meeting of Rare Minds* in the book *Atom and Archetype – The Pauli/Jung Letters, 1932-1958* by Beverley Zabriskie: http://www.pupress.princeton.edu/titles/7042.html

The Collaborative Concentric Networking Model (Michael Pockocky) – Intuitive Life blog Dave Taylor:
http://www.intuitive.com/blog/rethinking_online_professional_networking.html

The Cluetrain Manifesto: http://www.cluetrain.com/

Chapter 15

Technorati: www.technorati.com

Google Blogsearch: http://blogsearch.google.com/

Blogs will Change your Business, Business Week May 2005: http://www.businessweek.com/magazine/content/05_18/b3931001_mz001.htm

Computerworld: http://www.computerworld.com/

Chapter 16

BNI: http://www.bni.com/

NRG: http://www.nrg-networks.co.uk/

BRE: http://www.brenet.co.uk/

Talaka: http://www.talaka.co.uk/

Chapter 17

The James Martin 21st Century School, Oxford University:
http://www.21school.ox.ac.uk/

What is Enlightenment magazine: http://www.wie.org/

The Life Learning Project, Alex Goodall: http://www.tllp.org/

Books referenced in the writing of this book.
(A more extensive reading list for the subject will be found at www.
afriendineverycity.com)

The World is Flat, A Brief History of the Globalised World in the 21st Century
Thomas Friedman (Penguin, Allen Lane)

We the media – grass roots journalism by the people for the people,
Dan Gillmor (O'Reilly)

Blog – understanding the information reformation that's changing your world
Hugh Hewitt (Nelson)

How art made the world Nigel Spivey (BBC Books)

Blink: The Power of Thinking Without Thinking Malcolm Gladwell (Little, Brown)

A Whole New Mind – Moving from the Information Age to the Conceptual Age
Daniel H. Pink (Riverhead Books)

The Selfish Gene Richard Dawkins (Oxford University Press)

The Spirit of Success – How to Connect Your Heart to Your Head in Work and Life
Norman Drummond (Hodder Mobius)

The Meme Machine Susan Blackmore (Oxford University Press)

Wink and Grow Rich – A Step-by-Step Guide To Making a Lot of Money
Roger Hamilton (www.rogerhamilton.com)

Principles of marketing, Philip Kotler (Prentice-Hall)

*The Wisdom of Crowds: Why the Many are Smarter Than the Few and How Collective
Wisdom Shapes Business, Economies, Societies and Nations*
James Surowiecki (Doubleday)

Emergence: The Connected Lives of Ants, Brains, Cities and Software
Steven Johnson (Scribner)

*A Theory of Everything: An Integral Vision for Business, Politics, Science and
Spirituality,* Ken Wilber (Shambhala)

Bowling Alone: The Collapse and Revival of American Community
Robert D. Putnam (Simon & Schuster)

Servant Leadership: A Journey into the Nature of Legitimate Power and Greatness
Robert K. Greenleaf, Larry C. Spears, Stephen R. Covey (Paulist Press)

Six Degrees: The Science of a Connected Age
Duncan J. Watts (W. W. Norton & Company)

The Cluetrain Manifesto: The End of Business as Usual
Christopher Locke, Rick Levine, Doc Searls, David Weinberger
(Perseus Publishing)

The Experience Economy B. Joseph Pine, James H. Gilmore, B. Joseph Pine II
(Harvard Business School Press)

The Hidden Power of Social Networks: Understanding How Work Really Gets Done in Organisations Rob Cross,
Andrew Parker, Robert L. Cross (Harvard Business School Press)

The Medium is the Message Marshall McLuhan, Quentin Fiore (Gingko Press)

The Tipping Point: How Little Things Can Make a Big Difference
Malcolm Gladwell (Back Bay Books)

Winning by Sharing Léon Benjamin (Business for Good)

The Empty Raincoat Charles Handy (Arrow Business Books)

Social Capital David Halpern (polity)

The Celestine Prophecy James Redfield (Bantam Books)

Now, Discover your Strengths Marcus Buckingham, Donald O. Clifton (Free Press)

The Phenomenon of Man Pierre Teilhard de Chardin (Perennial)

The Different Drum M. Scott Peck (Arrow Books)

Index

Symbols

Printed in the United Kingdom
by Lightning Source UK Ltd.
111842UKS00001B/169-318